Society & Culture
Undergraduate Research Forum

Within the Shadow of Giants

Spring 2015

Volume 7

CHIEF FORUM COORDINATOR
Alexander Coburn

JOURNAL TEAM
Tania Ryan   Editor
Amy Villasenor   Junior Editor
Madison Long   Assistant Editor

COMMITTEE MEMBERS
Madison Long   Secretary & Treasurer
Lauren Russ   Webmistress
Horacio Arcila   Publicity
Doshia Caradine   Catering and Event Planner

FACULTY ADVISORS
Alexis T. Boutin, Ph.D.
Richard J. Senghas, Ph.D.

SOCIETY AND CULTURE UNDERGRADUATE RESEARCH FORUM
Sonoma State University
1801 East Cotati Avenue
Stevenson Hall 2054
Rohnert Park, CA 94928

Email inquiries to: scurfssu@gmail.com

All works within this volume are also available digitally via the
Sonoma State University Library Scholarworks program.

Original Front Cover Image provided by Alex Coburn
Cover Design and Journal Layout by Tania Ryan

THE SOCIETY AND CULTURE UNDERGRADUATE RESEARCH FORUM
PUBLISHED VOLUME LISTING

VOLUME	TITLE / THEME	YEAR	ISBN
1	VOLUME 1	2009	5800030992673
2	VOLUME 2	2010	5800046136818
3	CULTURE	2011	9781463586003
4	CROSSING BOUNDARIES	2012	9781477406458
5	WATERWORKS	2013	9781484935255
6	IMPRINTS	2014	9781312204676
7	WITHIN THE SHADOW OF GIANTS	2015	9781329136502

Available at http://lulu.com/spotlight/SCURF
or on Amazon, Barnes and Noble, or Ingram Content Group

CONTENTS

iii   Acknowledgements & Special Recognition

v   Foreword   *John Wingard, Ph.D.*

IN THE SHADOW OF GIANTS

1   A Giant of Languages: The Impacts of English Lingua Franca on Interactions Between Native and Non-Native Speakers in Sweden   Helen Sinor

15   Finding the Third Space: A Frontier for Future Foreign Language Learning   Hilary Honnold

29   An Application for Revitalization: Sonoma County's Pomo Languages   Emma Zornes

41   English and It's Affects on Global Music   Katelyn Kinder

53   Undocumented Latino Students in Higher Education   Griselda Madrigal Lara

71   Doing & Undoing Microaggressions: Power and Privilege in Day-to-Day Campus   Nanette Reyes Cruz

83   The Tool Box: Researching discourse around conflict management paradigms   Paulina Ceja

97   Terrorism in the Modern World: The Changing Definition of Terrorism and its Implications   Melissa Ritchey

111   Nuclear Power Discourse: Why Bodega Bay residents needed Nuclear Power like a Hole in the Head   Melissa McLees

125   Captive Mandrills' Core Behavioral Needs at the San Francisco Zoo: A Need for Behavioral Enrichment   Kyle Runzel

141   Enclosure Use in a Captive All-Male Group of Squirrel Monkeys (Saimiri sciureus)   Madeline Warnement

—

TECHNOLOGY HIGH

155 Forward for Technology High   *Lauren Russ &*
Horacio Arcila

157 Do Childhood Traumas Result in Adult   Molly Melville
Disorders? Celebrity Case Studies

175 The Different Aspects of Growth Enhancers   Zachary Miller
that Affect a Variety of Plants Growth

189 Analyzing Origins and Effects of Gender   Marcos Carballal
Stereotypes within Testing Environments

201 Afterword   *Karin Jaffe Ph.D.*

205 Photos from the 7th Annual Society & Culture Undergraduate
Research Forum on April 15th 2015

ACKNOWLEDGEMENTS

The 2015 Planning Committee of the Society & Culture Undergraduate Research Forum is very grateful for the support of numerous people and organizations. SCURF was generously funded this year by Sonoma State students' Instructionally Related Activity fees.

We thank Mark and Terri Stark of Stark Reality Restaurants for donating gift cards to the best oral presentation and poster award winners. We also thank Dr. Rubin Armiñana, President of Sonoma State University, Dr. Andrew Rogerson, Provost and Vice President for Academic Affairs, and Dr. John Wingard, Interim Dean of the School of Social Sciences, for their continued support. We also gratefully acknowledge and thank both Dr. John Wingard and Dr. Karin Jaffe (Chair, Anthropology Department) for agreeing to provide the Foreword and Afterword that thoughtfully bookend this volume.

We are very much obliged to Dr. Bonnie Clark (University of Denver), this year's keynote speaker for her powerful presentation, "Student Research and Community Engagement: A View from the Amache Internment Camp Project."

Daniel Smith, Director of the Office of Undergraduate Research, invited SCURF to participate in the 1st annual SSU Research Symposium and gave generously of his time to ensure that our integration was seamless.

Finally, we would like to acknowledge Dr. Alexis Boutin and Dr. Richard Senghas, our SCURF Advisors, whose guidance, counsel, and wisdom saw us through our seventh SCURF event.

~ The Society and Culture Undergraduate Research Team

SPECIAL RECOGNITION

Our annual presenter prizes were awarded at the SCURF conference for best oral presentation and best poster presentation. We would like to thank our esteemed judges for their time and careful attention, and would like to congratulate the winners as follows:

Helen Sinor Best Oral Presentation

Macy McClung Best Poster Presentation

PRESENTATION WINNERS

Macy McClung *(left)*
Helen Sinor *(right)*

JUDGES

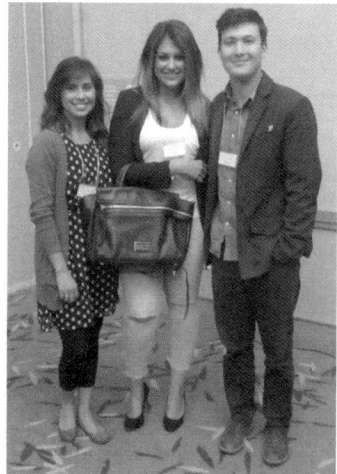

Meagan Horeczko (left)
Teagan Kiefer *(center)*
Tomio Endo *(right)*

JUDGES

Teagan Kiefer   Meagan Horeczko

Tomio Endo   Sandra Massey   *(not shown)*

FOREWORD

This year marks the seventh year for the Society and Culture Undergraduate Research Forum (SCURF). Given that seven is one of the most marked numbers across human cultures, occurring in religion, sports, music, and many other domains of human activity, this is something of a milestone volume for SCURF. Beyond its symbolic significance, it also reflects seven very successful years of an endeavor initiated by a small group of innovative and motivated students. Following in their footsteps, many more hard working students have not only sustained the efforts of the initial group, but have continued to develop and build upon the original concept.

Not only has the number of participants grown, but the breadth of papers has also increased. The original papers primarily reflected the research of students in the Department of Anthropology. Since then, SCURF has attracted the research of students from many other disciplines, including Global Studies, Psychology, History, Philosophy, and Biology, to name but a few. It has also grown in sophistication. Initially a somewhat eclectic collection of papers, subsequent volumes carried such interdisciplinary themes as Crossing Boundaries, Waterworks, Humanity's Imprint on Time and Space, and this year's theme Within the Shadow of Giants.

SCURF continues to be on the cutting edge of two trends growing rapidly, not only at Sonoma State University, but also across academia: student generated research and interdisciplinarity. It is not surprising that these two things go together. Today's students, and the students whose papers appear in this volume, have greater access to the massive amounts of information that reflect the cumulative efforts of generations of scholars. Given this access, it is not surprising that these students are discovering linkages across the disciplines, beyond even those of their teachers. Nor is it surprising that the research would find an outlet in a student-led project such as SCURF.

Beyond being an outlet for cutting edge and interdisciplinary research, the students who organize the SCURF symposium and publish this research are developing important skills they will carry with them after they graduate and move onto the next stages of their careers.

Finally, I want commend the faculty who provide the guidance and inspiration necessary to develop the scholarship reflected in the papers appearing in this volume.

John H. Wingard, Ph.D.
Dean, School of Social Sciences
Sonoma State University

WITHIN THE SHADOW OF GIANTS

A GIANT OF LANGUAGES: THE IMPACTS OF ENGLISH LINGUA FRANCA ON INTERACTIONS BETWEEN NATIVE AND NON-NATIVE ENGLISH SPEAKERS IN SWEDEN

HELEN SINOR

ANTHROPOLOGY AND PHILOSOPHY

SONOMA STATE UNIVERSITY

ABSTRACT

This study discusses the effects that English Lingua Franca (ELF) has on the interactions between Swedish university students and international students who come to Sweden. Many international students do not become fluent, or even proficient, in the native language during their time in Sweden. Instead they prefer to communicate in English, which eliminates one of the advertised benefits of studying abroad: learning a second language. Uppsala University in Sweden has a high level of international students who often congregate at the student nations, which are student-run restaurants, pubs, and clubs. The sample group consists primarily of Swedish club workers at these nations who have a high level of interaction using English with incoming international students year after year. English has emerged, for better or worse, as the dominant lingua franca used around the globe. It has become a giant of languages, greatly affecting all those put under its shadow. Globalization has expedited the spread of ELF, increasing the need for research into the effects of this phenomenon. It is especially common in many countries in Europe for English to be taught as a second language in grade schools and throughout higher education. Scandinavia has some of the highest rates of English speakers in Europe, making it a well-suited place to study the interactions between native and non-native speakers.

Key Words: Lingua Franca, English, International, ELF, Students, Globalization

Globalization is bringing communities together around the world and with it, second language learning. Students who participate in study abroad programs at universities are strongly encouraged to study the native language of the country they are traveling to in order to facilitate their integration into the local community. Notably, where there is a high the rate of English speakers in the country, there seems to be a much lower rate of students who actually become proficient in a second language, which may have an effect on students' experience abroad. Through the analysis of data collected from a selection of native Swedes who have a high level of contact with international students, it does not appear that they expect international students to learn Swedish. Additionally, using English does not explicitly affect their relationships with internationals.

Foreign and second language learning exploded worldwide in the 1950s, heralding the rise of English as a global lingua franca (Phillipson, 2008, p. 335). However, research on this phenomenon did not hit full swing until the early 1990s (Pakir, 2009, p. 229). The terms *World Englishes* (WE), *English Lingua Franca* (ELF), and *International English* (IE) entered into the academic vocabulary around this time. Seidlhofer (2005) defines English lingua franca as "a way of referring to communication in English between speakers with different first languages" (p. 339). World English is considered an umbrella term, generally referring to "nativized" or indigenized varieties of English. International English, on the other hand, is a somewhat antiquated word used to describe the more prescriptive ideal of English which is written and spoken by "educated" speakers of the language. That is to say, IE refers to the kind of English that is transmitted through "formal" education to foreign or second language learners (Pakir, 2009, p. 225). English Lingua Franca (ELF) will be used in the following study to describe the general use of English abroad.

Discussions of globalization and ELF have increasingly raised questions about the potential political, social, and economic impact of the phenomenon. Phillipson (2008) has been one of the dominant researchers voicing his concerns about linguistic imperialism which, as he puts it, "interlocks with the neoliberal economy, finance, the military, culture, and education" (p. 337). He argues that TESOL (Teachers of English to Speakers of Other Languages) is placing English at the top of a linguistic hierarchy, where the US also currently rests as a "model for the world." He goes on to relate this to the idea that the spread of English as a lingua franca is affiliated with the agendas of those dominating this hierarchy (Phillipson, 2008, p. 336). The effects of global hierarchies on concepts surrounding second language learning and ideas regarding the value of a language have emerged as relevant factors regarding Swedish students' views on ELF.

Much of the most recent research done on ELF focuses on second language learning and the use of English as a contact language between non-native speakers. As language is acknowledged as a core element in the creation and negotiation of identity, the spread of ELF has incited a lot of interest into concepts of identity with regard to second language learning as well as interactions using ELF (see Gnutzmann et al., 2014; Sung, 2014). Gnutzmann et al.'s (2014) recognition that "students' views can be seen as an indicator of linguistic and social change" (p. 444) explains why students are the optimal target population of their study. This notion is utilized in the following research as well, as students who are participating in the study abroad program are representative of current globalizing phenomena and changing interactions between native and non-native English speakers.

Research into the effects of studying abroad on second language learning began sporadically in the 1960s through the use of language test scores (see Carroll, 1967). Later on, throughout the 1980s and 1990s, researchers began utilizing new methods, including the ACTFL/ILR Oral Proficiency Interview (OPI) (Freed, 1998, p.

34). Freed's (1998) analysis of multiple studies reveals that students who participate in study abroad programs achieve higher levels of second language proficiency when compared with those who do not, however many of the tests used in these studies do not capture a sufficiently nuanced, qualitative understanding of this topic (p. 35). DeKeyser (1991) conducted a study which, apart from failing to identify a major difference in language learning in the classroom as opposed to abroad, determined that studying abroad "had a strong impact on the way the learners were perceived by native speakers" (p. 115). This finding ties into the idea of linguistic relativity, which refers to the theory that grammar has an impact on how individuals evaluate reality, thereby impacting their general worldview (Whorf, 1941/1956, p. 221). Bylund 2014 offers an illuminating discussion regarding the connection between linguistic relativity and second language acquisition. These studies form a foundation from which the topic of this paper stems, however, the subjects of study are not the second language learners themselves, but the native speakers who come into contact with international students while they are abroad.

METHODS/DEMOGRAPHICS: SKYPING WITH SWEDISH STUDENTS

A series of in-depth interviews have been conducted with four participants; a necessarily small group due to time and resource constraints. The interviewees are native Swedes, all of which are fluent in both Swedish and English and have a high level of contact with international students (daily/weekly). The participants – chosen because of previous interactions with the researcher involving conversations about second language learning abroad – were contacted via social media. The interviews took place over Skype and were digitally recorded.

The data from the interviews are categorized according to trends that were identified post-collection. Many of the participants had similar responses that have been placed into sections, such as: feelings about the benefits of a second language, what circumstances compel internationals to learn Swedish, and which languages they thought were more valuable to study than others. Globalization and entertainment were among topics that came up spontaneously during multiple interviews. These are not part of the original topics in the study but, as they emerged repeatedly throughout the interview process, a discussion of the entertainment industry and globalization became necessary for the study.

The participants are all native Swedes, between the ages of 23 and 30, who live in Uppsala and attend Uppsala University. Half of the interviewees are members of Södermanlands Nerikes Nation, a student-run pub where many internationals come into contact with Swedes, either through work or recreation. The other half live in Flogsta, a student housing area that accommodates many international students who study abroad in Uppsala. All participants have a high level of interaction with international students, and primarily use English as their medium of communication. Each interviewee uses English on a daily basis for various activities including: interpersonal communication, reading online articles, watching TV shows and movies, or listening to English music. All identify as being fluent both in Swedish and English.

As an international student in Uppsala, I lived in Flogsta and was a member of Södermanlands Nerikes Nation. Flogsta is primarily made up of international students who stay for a six to twelve months and then return to their home countries. The Swedish students who live there have often shared the communal corridors with multiple "generations" of international students. Södermanlands Nerikes Nation (commonly referred to as Snerikes) is one of thirteen student nations, some of which have been affiliated with Uppsala University since the 17th century. They began as clubs for students who came from the same province to gather, and have since evolved into sophisticated student-run restaurants, pubs, and clubs. Each nation has a unique personality and appeal, for Snerikes their particularly strong preservation of traditional customs and values draws in Swedes and internationals alike. After several months of working at Snerikes, I ran for and was elected to the position of Helgfika Höst. I managed and planned a weekly brunch at the restaurant with four other individuals, also becoming involved in many of the most traditional aspects of nation life, which allowed me to observe the inner workings of these customs and how they are perceived both by Swedes and internationals.

FINDINGS

INCENTIVES FOR SECOND LANGUAGE ACQUISITION ABROAD

One of the greatest benefits that is advertised to students looking into the study abroad program is learning a second language. Second language learning is a widely researched topic with many studies focusing on the teaching of dominant languages to minority groups, the preservation of endangered languages, and globalization. The participants of this study reflect the view that speaking a second language has certain benefits, relating the great effect that speaking English has had on their lives. It is their main method of communication with the world beyond Sweden. One participant related that is hugely beneficial for applying for jobs and in school. Another responded that speaking English had added to his personal and intellectual growth:

> I think that studying more than one language makes you really reflect on how you speak and the way in which you speak because the difference between formal English and formal Swedish is pretty big, so when you try to use one and translate into the other you get to think about your way of expressing yourself. I also think that learning more than one language is an incentive to evolve your vocabulary. Because I'll come across a word in English that I don't know, I'll look it up every

single time and sometimes I don't even know the word in Swedish so I have to look that up and so I've had a nice bit of learning, and I do this regularly.

Another participant, when asked about whether he thought that everyone should learn a second language, responded:

> I think that people should have a second language, because if you only speak your native language it's going be so much harder to break barriers and learn about other cultures. If you are a native speaker in English you have a great advantage and I guess that's a reason not to learn a second language, but if you're a Swede you really need a second language, and English is the preferable one, or Spanish.

This response brings up the question of whether native English speakers have the advantage, or if the opposite is true. The rate of bilingualism in the US has been on the rise – though we are still at less than 25% of the total population – and involves a very diverse range of languages (Shin & Kominski, 2010, pp. 2-4). Still, there are concerns as to whether or not the US is falling behind, with Obama himself suggesting at a 2008 rally that, "we should have every child speaking more than one language" (Obama, 2008). The European Union, in comparison, has been promoting the study of not one, but two foreign languages (Gnutzmann et al., 2014, p. 450). As globalization has greatly increased the need for cultural cooperation, the benefits of multilingualism affect not only the individual but society as a whole.

WHO *DOES* LEARN SWEDISH? : FEW INTERNATIONAL STUDENTS

The most conclusive and across-the-board responses in the interviews are that very few internationals learn Swedish. Some of the responses were:

I don't think I've met an American student that actively tries to learn and use Swedish.

I don't think a lot of people learn Swedish at all.

Really few people learn and use Swedish, only one guy I know still uses Swedish. Some people still know some phrases but other than that I don't really know anyone that really uses Swedish.

Three out of four participants expressed the opinion that it is unnecessary to learn Swedish, and they are impressed and surprised when they meet someone who is actually trying to speak Swedish regularly. Half of the respondents replied that they would be willing to speak Swedish with an international who was trying to practice, but only under certain circumstances. In the student nations, when workers need to be focused on the tasks at hand, it is essential to use English in order to be understood and work together efficiently. The other half replied that they do not have the patience to struggle through a conversation with someone who is trying to learn Swedish, they would much rather use English. The one circumstance in which it is agreed that a person necessarily should learn Swedish, is if they are planning on becoming a Swedish resident. The interviews revealed that the few international students who do learn Swedish tend to have a closer connection to Sweden than most, such as: having Swedish heritage, or entering into a relationship with a Swede.

USING ELF IN SWEDEN

One of the biggest incentives to learn Swedish while abroad is the chance that students might avoid missing something by only using English. However, even with this in mind, none of the participants of the study declared that they thought that international students should use Swedish primarily, instead of ELF. Only one interviewee discussed a situation in which Swedish should be used instead of English.

> There is a slight sort of resistance to speaking English, especially with some of the more traditional nation values, such as during landskåp and gasques, because the traditions that we hold are Swedish and doesn't really translate into English. But as far as individual contact – person to person – I don't really think there is a difference.

Two participants, who are not as integrated into the nation culture, stated that learning Swedish would not have a big impact on international student's experience while in Sweden:

> I think most Swedes are not very traditional in that sense, to make a big deal out of the culture. So many Swedes already speak English, even if they are older and not fluent they can speak English well enough to communicate with students.

> If they want to stay here and get a job then it would be better if they learned Swedish but I don't think that only speaking English really affects their interactions with Swedes because we all speak English well.

Notably, there are differences between the response from the nation-worker, and the responses from those who are not strongly affiliated with a nation. Two participants brought up the idea of tradition in regards to the use of ELF, but in different contexts. They both see the idea that Swedish should be used instead of ELF as very traditional, but only one of them brings up a situation in which a tradition necessitates the use of Swedish alone.

TECHNOLOGY, ENTERTAINMENT, AND THE SPREAD OF ELF

Several participants discussed the effect that technology and entertainment has had on the spread of ELF and their own use of English. One participant stated that even if he does not speak English every day, he is constantly reading articles online that are in English, and watching TV series that are not dubbed. For another participant, whether or not movies are dubbed is a big factor in the spread of English across Europe:

> It [ELF] has to do with pop culture and the entertainment industry that comes to Sweden. Also, one of the reasons Swedes learn English is because we don't dub our movies, so even as a young kid you'll start to pick up English from movies. In Europe, Scandinavian countries and the Netherlands are the countries that don't dub the movies and in those countries you'll find the biggest amount of English speakers, so I think that one relates to another.

CONCLUDING THOUGHTS

Although the group taking part in this study is in no way representative of the entire student population in Uppsala, there are a few common trends that point towards some preliminary conclusions. Firstly, there are many benefits to speaking more than one language, as reflected in social policies across the world (Obama, 2008; Gnutzmann et al., 2014, p. 450), and as recognized by the participants in this study. However, there are differences in which languages are seen as more valuable to speak. Global hierarchies, as Phillipson 2008 suggests, appear to have led many students to the conclusion that certain languages are simply less useful than others. Swedish falls under this category of languages, even to native Swedes. One of the respondents questioned why anyone not living in Sweden would want to speak Swedish, stating that it is not a "world language."

Additionally, Swedish students do not tend to see themselves as especially "traditional." They have various customs that they celebrate and uphold that are uniquely Swedish. However, in their day to day life they do not share particularly strong nationalistic tendencies which would create a general aversion to using ELF. Finally, Swedish students do not tend to explicitly change the way they act around an international student who has not made an effort to learn Swedish. Indirectly, however, international students may feel excluded from the more traditional aspects of Swedish life (such as events at the nations) because these aspects of student life are performed strictly in Swedish.

WHAT NEXT?

The findings presented in this study illuminate several possible cultural tendencies, which merit future investigation. First, there is the issue of ELF; are native English speakers at a disadvantage (due, ironically, to a perceived advantage) because they are not effectively challenged to learn a second language? This in turn, brings up the question of how valuable it truly is to speak a second language; how do we quantify the benefits of second language learning? Finally, what are the effects of global hierarchies on second language learning? These are but a few of the questions that this study just barely breached, but could be next steps to expanding our knowledge of second language acquisition, ELF, and globalization.

REFERENCES

Bylund, E., & Athanasopoulos, P. (2014). Linguistic relativity in SLA : Toward a new research program. *Language Learning, 64,* 4. doi :10.1111/lang.12080

Carroll, J.B. (1967). Foreign language proficiency levels attained by language majors near graduation from college. *Foreign Language Annals, 1,* 131-151.

DeKeyser, R. (1991). Foreign language development during a semester abroad. *Foreign Language Acquisition Research and the Classroom* ed. By B. Freed, 104-119. Lexington, Mass.: D. C. Health & Co.

Freed, B., Lazar, N., & So, S. (1998). Fluency in writing: Are there differences between students who have studied abroad and those who have not? Presented at the annual meeting of the Modern Language Association. December, 1998. San Francisco, CA.

Gnutzmann, C., Jakisch, J., & Rabe, F. (2014). English as a lingua franca: A source of identity for young Europeans? *Multilingua, 33,* 3-4. doi:10.1515/multi-2014-0020

Obama, B. (Speaker). (2008, July 8). Barack Obama: Your children should learn to speak Spanish. Retrieved from https://www.youtube.com/watch?v=BZprtPat1Vk

Pakir, A. (2009). English as a lingua franca: Analyzing research frameworks in International English, World Englishes and ELF. *World Englishes, 28, 2* doi:10.1111/j.1467-971X.2009.01585.x

Phillipson, R. (2008). Lingua franca or lingua frankensteinia? English in European integration and globalisation. *World Englishes, 27, 2* doi: 10.1111/j.1467-971X.2008.00555.x

Seidlhofer, Barbara. (2005). English as a lingua franca. *ELT Journal, 59,* 4 doi:10.1093/elt/cci064

Shin, Hyon B., & Kominski, R. A. (2010). *Language use in the United States: 2007.* American Community Survey Reports, ACS-12. U.S. Census Bureau, Washington, DC.

Sung, C. C. M. (2014). English as a lingua franca and global identities: Perspectives from four second language learners of English in Hong Kong. *Linguistics and Education, 26* doi:10.1080/07908318.2014.890210

Whorf, B. L. (1941/1956). *Language, thought, and reality: Selected writings of Benjamin Lee Whorf* (J. B. Carroll, Ed.; 2nd ed.). Cambridge, MA: MIT Press.

FINDING THE THIRD SPACE:
A FRONTIER FOR FUTURE FOREIGN LANGUAGE LEARNING

HILARY HONNOLD

HUMAN DEVELOPMENT MAJOR

SONOMA STATE UNIVERSITY

ABSTRACT

For the last several generations there have been two spaces for learning language, home and school/work. Emerging in the recent generation of the millennials, there has been an emergence of a third space. This third space is messaging, social media, and gaming. A combination of these have lead to evolving word usage and even new words. In this realm I would like to explore when, why and how this happens. Pervious studies have focused on each category separately through various research methods, most commonly survey. Unlike most articles found, I seek to find a connection between each domain. My main source of data collection will be searching popular hashtags or topics on Twitter, Tumblr and gaming sites such as PCGamer. Once data are collected I will be looking for patterns in words and morphemes created by each domain. Through this I will be able to see how has language evolved in recent years. If there are patterns that are typical, what these patterns suggest and will they show something about our general worldview. If there is a conciseness of a general worldview of our online culture in the United States, do other cultures use the same online lexicon.

Key Words: Millennial, Technology, Third Space,
Case-Base Learning, Social Media, Education

During the last several generations there have been two spaces for learning language: home and school/work. Emerging in the recent generations there has been an emergence of a third space. This third space is messaging, social media sites, and gaming. This term came from Robert Godwin-Jones (2005). Currently this is the fastest growing form of communication and includes, but not limited to Facebook, Instagram, Twitter, Tumblr, and gaming sites like PCGamer. Almost everyone uses some form of social media, only fifteen percent of adults do not, but it is largely dominated by the millennial generation, people born between approximately 1982-1999 (Zickuhr, 2013). This project was inspired by a detailed account of the third space used a future language learning source conducted by Godwin-Jones (2005). Due to the fast pace of technological growth, the article is now dated, I seek to update and add to his work with the expansion into social media sites. Social media sites have encouraged the evolution word usage and even the creation of new words. I would like to explore when, and how this happens in the new realm of the third space. Pervious studies have focused on each category separately through various methods, most commonly utilizing survey techniques. Unlike most currently published articles, I seek to find a connection between each domain. With this connection between each domain I plan to propose a change in how language is being taught for generation to come.

First, I set out to define who the millennia's are as a generation and why they are important, to help my understanding beyond what I assume as a millennial myself. I found a very interesting article by an anonymous source that outlines what makes up a millennial (Anonymous, 2001). While I found the article interesting, it not a credible source however, it turned out to be a book review of a creditable book written by historians Neil Howe and Bill Strauss (Howe & Strauss, 2000). Howe and Strauss define a millennial is a person born between the years 1982-1998. Howe and

Strauss based their research on surveys and have an extensive background of analyzing the life expectancies of America's generations. The book claims that during the time baby boomers were being raised, families were beginning to crumble, this was followed by Generation X, where family stability fell, leading to the parents of Millennia's to tighten up and watch over their children nonstop, resulting in a new found appreciation for the family unit. As a byproduct, millennial children are by far more confident in themselves than pervious generations (Howe & Strauss, 2000, pp.325-376). The book also states that this generation is more numerous, affluent, ethnically diverse, and better educated than the generations before them (Howe & Strauss, 2000,p.4). Which is true and could be shown with population charts I believe. The authors' claims that this is a combination for the next greatest American generation since WWII, but cannot be until they are tested with a big issue like a war or an economic downfall (Howe & Strauss, 2000, pp.323, 324). The book in this sense is a bit dated because 9/11 had not happen or the economic crash of 2008. Although maybe that is not applicable to the millennial generation as a test but a foundation for learning since most were still children through these events.

Another way to look at the millennial generation is by looking at their current political beliefs. Gillespie (2014) wrote about this based off research conducted by the Reason Foundation and the Rupe Foundation, which contained nearly 2,400 representative from the millennial generation (Gillespie, 2014). When a millennial is asked to identify with a political party, 62% of them say liberal, but this is because they believe that being liberal means supporting gay marriage and legalizing marijuana, they do not relate it to government spending, as past generations have done when identifying with a party (Gillespie, 2014). Another interesting finding in the survey of political terms is that 42% of millennials actually prefer socialism but only 16% could correctly define the term (Gillespie, 2014). The

Gillespie goes on to talk about how baby boomers and generations in between are generally the same but with a different vocabulary than millennials, such as free market instead capitalism, the only difference in generations is that millennials will put culture before politics (Gillespie, 2014).

Keeping in mind what a millennial is, lets look into what is Godwin-Jones (2005) 'third space' is and how it relates to language learning. A disclaimer though, is it is somewhat dated due to how fast the Internet and technology change. In this paper, Godwin-Jones (2005) defined the third space as the area for learning online using such things such as online gaming, peer-to-peer sharing, and instant messaging, in updated terms this is social media (Godwin-Jones, 2005,p.17). Unlike other articles addressing online learning, this one gives credit to the multiple ways online language learning is useful, for example; computer literacy, community building, identity creation, collaborative learning, or even mentoring through helping others with game related strategies (Godwin-Jones, 2005,p.17).

The first portion of Godwin-Jones (2005) deals with messaging. This was probably the most dated section because it deals with defining what IM is and how it is gaining popularity. Today, very few people use the original IM modality but instead now use SMS, which at the time this article was written had just begun being used in the USA and was widely used in Europe and Asia already (Godwin-Jones, 2005,p.17). The Godwin-Jones (2005) does state that this is due to the fact that texting on phones is more difficult than typing on a computer, and needs improvement along with a more sophisticated speech/text tools (Godwin-Jones, 2005). This of course, is no longer an issue with mobile technology ten years later. Though this did not stop several research companies of the time to work within this realm to create applications for language use. An example is Java-based exercises from Great Britain. At the time of the article Nokia, was the leading mobile phone vendor, and had about twenty cell phone models that supported Java (Godwin-Jones, 2005,p.18). Today almost every smart phone you can get your hands on has this capability, among other advancements. Discussed in this section as well was moblogging. This term essentially means, blogging on a mobile device (Godwin-Jones, 2005,p.18). This term did not stick, but is still highly relevant in today's society. Noted in this section of Godwin-Jones was also emailing, which is still commonly used today.

The second section is on peer-to-peer sharing. Highlights from this section include the invention of the iPod, sharing music, and the friendly byproduct of MP3 format. While there might be several legal issues with music, as there still are today, the handiness of the MP3 file still remains. Godwin-Jones states that several sites began to offer beginning language learning through the use of MP3 download and in fact this is still true (Godwin-Jones, 2005,p.19). Godwin-Jones suggests in this section that peer-to-peer file sharing should be used more commonly. This still remains problematic to this day, because of copyright infringements.

The final section is on online gaming. The article references several leaders such as Rebecca Black who studied how online gaming communities for anime are often communicated in English even though they are from Chinese and Japanese backgrounds (Godwin-Jones, 2005,p.20). Gaming is often overlooked as a language-learning outlet because it tends to have the sigma associated with vast amounts of times wasted (Godwin-Jones, 2005,p.20). This is not necessarily the truth anymore, as the article points out that several company are investing money to exploit this uncharted territory, among them is the U.S. military who have made serious games such as mission rehearsal exercises (Godwin-Jones, 2005,p.20). Another great example is a game created for children to teach English, its premise is using English to help fix a spaceship to get off an alien planet and return home (Goodwin-Jones, 2005,p.20). Today you can see evidence that this idea has been continually developed with sites like playinfluent.com that allows you to play interactive games and learn a language at the same time. While Godwin-Jones maybe somewhat dated, it still makes some valid points, including that everything is constantly evolving and technology is a force to be recognized when it comes to educational value.

If this article was written in current times it would have a large section devoted to social media sites like; Tumblr, Twitter, Facebook, Pinterest, Reddit, Snapchat, and many more. Like other third space domains, social media would be a useful outlet for foreign language use practices. Can you imagine having a class Tumblr page that students contributed to? This leads to my personal research. Where I seek to find a connection between varying online domains to bridge an understanding of current language use. My expected results were to discover a language connection between different third space domains and to use the connection to give insight into how millennia's are learning/using language. The results of my analysis will help adjust techniques in learning for future generations to come.

My main method for data collection was looking at sites' top trending hashtags or topics depending on how the site is used. To achieve this I planned on following top accounts on each site and pulling the top twenty postings from each domain. Due to time restrictions, I picked three domains: Twitter, Tumbler, and PCGamer. From each site, I looked at their top trending topics of the day, took the top five and looked at those topics most recent five posts. In each area the most recent five posts were recorded exactly as they appeared online not editing or changing spelling/grammar issues to keep the integrity of the post. Due to me being fluent in only English, if there was a recent post in another language I skipped over it and went to the next. To analyze the data, I created a summative model. To do this I organize my data into structures or patterns as it is being collected. The purpose of the summative model is to refine and modify each category to find links or relations. When structures become clear; the data will emerge into a summative model (see table below), with varying levels of understanding (LeCompte & Schensul, 2010,p.205). In left to right of the table holds information of which domain, the top trending topic, a recent post, type of posting, whether it was them posting or someone else words and if they used personal pronouns or names.

Third Space: Domain	Top Trending Topics	Recent Postings	Initial Type	Original Content	Personal Pronouns and Names
Twitter	#earthday	We must take care of Mother Earth and she will take care of us. #Earthday	Personal	original	We, she, us
Tumblr	The Little Prince	It is only with the heart that one can see rightly; what is essential is invisible to the eye.	Pop Culture/ Literature	Quote	it is
PCGamer	Galactic Civilizations III	The UI looks terrible and the graphic style of the ships looks clunky and unimaginative. Unless the game mechanics underneath the hood are very satisfying I'm, not going near this one	Gaming/ Interest	original	I'm

The reason behind tracking personal pronouns and names comes from a psychological study containing seven studies on proving how self-talk matters (Kross et al, 2014). Kross and colleges argued that personal pronouns where linked to linguistic distancing connected to social anxiety (Kross et al, 2014:305). Due to the nature of Internet postings mainly being focused on 'self', I predicted this is most likely what I would find. Unfortunately because of a small sample size, I was not able to find any connection to this theory on social media. There was however a few things I did notice in my observations. It was common on both Twitter and Tumblr to have hashtags that added more insight into the post. For example, I observed someone post "shoutout to Barry Bonds for no longer being a convicted felon #NotEvenBeingSarcastic." If you were to read this without the hashtag you would assume they were being ironic. This is very different to gaming sites member communication because they tend to be either mentoring one another or expressing their opinions on content. Unfortunately, I did not find a linguistic tie I was looking for, only a culture that is self-oriented. Not in a bad way, just opinionated and maybe that is a tie to social anxiety. Looking forward if I was able to dedicate more time with a large sample size, it might be different.

Even though I did not find the linguistic connection I hoped for, I still think after studying social media there is a connection to future educational language program possibilities. Looking back at Godwin-Jones he stated the not only is it millennial generation but they are also the generation of "digital native" (Godwin-Jones, 2005,p.17). Millennial parents are known as "digital immigrants", because unlike their children whom the technology is second nature they had to adapt to technology (Godwin-Jones, 2005, p.17). It did not come natural. Recently there was a study done by Mondahl and Razmerita (2014), on foreign language learning using social media, collaboration, and social learning (Mondahl & Razmerita, 2014). To do this they developed a study where the control group learned in the typical way of classroom instructed foreign language courses, while the experimental group tackled language learning through Web 2.0 with case-based learning technique (Mondahl & Razmerita 2014,p.340). What is a case base learning technique? This is when learning is based on real life situations using media outlets. In order to do this, students must be familiar with theory and case material to do the task of deciphering the a assignment at hand and may include writing press releases, memos, analysis and even forum discussions (Mondahl & Razmerita 2014,p.342). The theory behind case-based language learning is that language is a construction process, and is put together through experiencing success or failures in situations, and accepting that personal involvement/motivation are key learning elements (Mondahl & Razmerita 2014, p.339).

To further their research, Mondahl and Razmerita included both quantitative and qualitative data retrieval. For quantitative data, they conducted closed questionnaires, pre-test results/grading, and post-test exam grades. For qualitative data they included open-ended questions and conducted focus group interviews. Interestingly, consistent with playing into how the millennials were raised to believe they were special, the experimental group gave more feedback because they had a higher level of interest due to the feeling that they brought something different to the table (Mondahl & Razmerita, 2014,p.347). This is supported by Howe and Strauss, when they speak of how millennials will not following blindly into their parents past trends, but instead are hopeful for future change (Howe & Strauss, 2000,p.6). The primary findings found that the experimental group was better at solving problems with written or verbal communication, and the control group was more successful at the linguistic level with syntax and morphology (Mondahl & Razmerita 2014,p.347). Although it was a through study, it should be looked into further with a larger sampling size to be taken as a serious pedagogy. Though it seems a healthy combination of both methods would be ideal. For example, a teacher could take Godwin-Jones advice and do a pen pal system (Godwin-Jones, 2005,p.17). If a teacher were to do this they could to a simple lesson no longer than twenty minutes and then have them use email to write something so their pen pals. This would be good to help them adapting between using formal and informal language. A teacher could get in contact with another teacher, in a different country, to aid with this activity.

This way their students will be force to really get into and learn a new language. Of course, the catch would be you can only reply to one another in the language you are unfamiliar with. This is just one of many possibilities.

The millennial's are a special generation with opportunities in technological advancements that past generation have never had. The concept of the third space is specifically unique to them. As digital native's they will be the groundbreakers for future generations. Mentoring them with the idea that they are 'special' and have something to bring to the table. Looking forward they should clue into this, to exploit the third space for teaching foreign languages.

REFERENCES

Anonymous (2001). The rise of the millennials. *FUTURIST*, *35*(2), 7. Retrieved March 20, 2015.

Bakewell, L. (2012). Madre: Perilous Journeys with a Spanish Noun. Albuquerque, New Mexico: University of New Mexico Press.

A Brief Introduction. (2015, January 1). Retrieved April 16, 2015,from http://playinfluent.com/

Davidson, E. (2011). Generation 1.5 -- a different kind of millennial student. Journal of Physician Assistant Education (Physician Assistant Education Association), 22(2), 13-19. Retrieved March 18, 2015

Gillespie, N. (2014, July 11). The Secret language of the Millennials. TIME.

Godwin-Jones, R. (2005). Messaging, gaming, peer-to-peer sharing: Language learning strategies & tools for the millennial generation. Language Learning & Technology, 9(1), 17-22. Retrieved March 17, 2015.

Howe, N., & Strauss, W. (2000). Millennials Rising: The Next Great Generation /By Neil Howe and Bill Strauss; Cartoons by R.J. Matson. New York: Vintage Books

Kross, E., Bruehlman-Senecal, E., Park, J., Burson, A., Dougherty, A. , Shablack, H., Bremner, R., & Moser, J. (2014). Self-talk as a regulatory mechanism: How you do it matters. Journal of Personality and Social Psychology, 106(2), 304-324. Retrieved March 28, 2015.

LeCompte,.& M Schensul, J., (2010). Data Analysis. In Designing & Conducting Ethnographic Research: An Introduction (2nd ed., p. 205). Lanham, Maryland: AltaMira Press.

Mondahl, M., & Razmerita, L. (2014). Social media, collaboration and social learning -- a case-study of foreign language learning. Electronic Journal of E-Learning, 12(4), 339-352. Retrieved April 1, 2015.

Newman, P., & Ratliff, M. (Eds.). (2001). Linguistic Fieldwork. Cambridge: Cambridge University Press.

Schensul, J., & LeCompte, M. (2013). Essential Ethnographic Methods: A Mixed Methods Approach (2nd ed.). Lanham, Maryland: AltaMira Press.

Zickuht, K. (2013). Who's not online and why. PewResearchCenter, 2-31. Retrieved April 28, 2015.

AN APPLICATION FOR REVITALIZATION: SONOMA COUNTY'S POMO LANGUAGES

EMMA ZORNES

ANTHROPOLOGY MAJOR

SONOMA STATE UNIVERSITY

ABSTRACT

Language is a facilitator that both bonds and divides many different peoples. In the case of the Pomo tribes of Northern California, much of the contact made between the non-native language speakers and the tribes have not been entirely successful. The California Indian Museum and Cultural Center and a group of software providers in Australia have teamed up to create an application for smart phones and tablets that plans to help revitalize the Pomo languages, specifically the Eastern, Southern, and Central variations. Working with existing linguistic data in physical and digital formats, informants and contributors to the database, and the CIMCC, this project aims to unearth the characteristics of language acquisition when applied to an application and to ensure transparency in how we use, store, share, and develop data that are provided to us though this new digital medium. This new digital medium, in the form of a software application, aims to bring together the many different branches of the Pomo languages, as well as the corresponding people and culture. Taking into account the historical components as well as the data coming from the CIMCC's application building process, this paper will address why and how language revitalization through this new medium may or not be the next beneficial step for the Pomo languages.

Key Words: Pomo Tribe, Language Acquisition, Technology, Linguistics, Mobile-Assisted

INTRODUCTION

An aboriginal language goes extinct every two weeks, according to the Miromaa Aboriginal Language and Technology Center (Miromaa, 2011). In the case of the Pomo tribes of California, this is especially relevant. All seven main Pomo language branches are endangered, and some are now even extinct (Norton, 2014). After hundreds of years of misinterpretation, cruelty, and suffering inflicted by the foreigners who wished to obtain the Natives' land, contemporary anthropologists wish to help revitalize and study the cultures that many once looked down upon. Focusing mainly on the Eastern Pomo, Southern Pomo, and Central Pomo languages, the California Indian Museum and Cultural Center (CIMCC), as well as students from the Sonoma State Department of Anthropology aim to develop an application for mobile devices which helps identify the phonological, phonetic, lexical, semantic, and pragmatic elements of the Pomo languages, including some of the differences among them (T. Endo, personal communication, February 26, 2015; CIMCC, 2013). Within this new learning medium there are many different benefits, criticisms, and methodologies.

BACKGROUND: POMO CULTURE

When learning and/or studying a language, understanding the culture behind the words is crucial. In the case of the Pomo tribes of California, this is especially true. Before much of the 1800s and 1900s California was home to many tribes, such as Pomo, Wiyot, Yurok, Hupa, Karuk, and Modoc peoples to name a few (Jacknis, 1996). As a precarious time in the history of the United States, the era of the Gold Rush was especially tough on the Native American peoples. Going from a world in which the boundaries consisted of rivers and land monuments to arbitrary lines drawn by the non-native settlers, and from groups of subsistence societies to one super-culture and language would be a large change for any group of peoples. Not only were the language and even body language different between the immigrant and the Native peoples, but world-view and perception differences led to an even larger realm of miscommunication to be present. As Norton (2014) uses as an example, the forceful and lusty men who came to mine without women would rape the women of the tribes, and when the families would attempt to confront the settlers about the indecency, they would be shot on sight. This example is typical of the initial relationships between the relatively recent immigrants and the indigenous peoples, including the Pomo (Norton, 2014).

Norton (2014, p.85) argues that in Western anthropology, ethnographers and historians have a long history of purposely nullifying and negating the suffering of other cultures and peoples as they pursue their own understanding. Now in the 21st century there is much less opportunity than there was in the time of the armchair anthropologists, yet there is often a foul connotation with the word "anthropologist" in the eyes of many Native people due to the centuries of abuse. According to research, the Pomo languages have gone though two distinct stages of bilingualism, first with Spanish and second with English. These two languages today are still the most spoken in the state while there is a large struggle to revitalize the seven branches of Pomo language (Ahlers, 2012, p.534). As a part of the newsletter *"News from Native California,"* Dublin (2010) presents a image of a school in which Kashaya Pomo is taught to the limited number of student participants. When a language is no longer needed or valued due to the primary language making it obsolete it is hard to obtain the attention of the youth who have the better language acquisition skills rather than adults (Loether, 2009). It is also worth mentioning that due to the mass genocide of Native American peoples, including the Pomo, most of the Native speakers are no longer able to teach the language (Norton, 2014). Many of the speakers are also particular about the voicing and spelling of their languages as it is personal to them (T. Endo, personal communication, February 26, 2015). This brings forward the question of what is to be done to revitalize a language in which there are few speakers and few members of the youth in the community actively wanting to learn the language of their ancestors? What new medium could bring together the old and the young to help revitalize the seven different branches of Pomo?

A NEW FORMAT FOR LANGUAGE ACQUISITION

Language is acquired though a number of mediums from birth to death. The traditional sources for this knowledge are parents and schools which are still one of the most common methods to learn a language (Loether, 2009). In this modern world there are a plethora of technological mediums to learn a language from. From Rosetta Stone to playing an online video game in which a different common tongue is used, language penetrates all realms of communication. Rosetta Stone is a very popular computer program in which a language is taught in a non traditional setting. By using similar aspects to the Miromaa, the program discussed in this paper, Rosetta Stone allows the freedom to learn at ones own pace and virtually anywhere with Internet access (Miromaa, 2011). However, Rosetta Stone does not exist to help revitalize languages and only offers many popular globalized languages (Rosetta, 2015). Though the California Indian Museum and Cultural Center is not the first to help revitalize a native language, it is still an exciting frontier for linguistics (Tribal College Journal, 2013). Working along side the Miromaa Aboriginal Language and Technology Center, CIMCC is using Miromaa's software to create an application for the Pomo Language (CIMCC, 2013). These applications plan to serve as a reference guide for basic words and phrases for the different languages (Tribal College Journal, 2013; CIMCC, 2013).

Using two differing examples of CALL (computer assisted language-learning) in two different contexts sheds some light on the struggles and triumphs of language acquisition in this new medium

(Özturan & Saricoban, 2013; Zhang et al., 2014). In one study, 82 Chinese students were taught English via CALL and the conclusive data derived from this study had little to do with which medium, listening versus CALL, worked better but that the key factor was motivation (Zhang et al., 2014). In the next, Özturan & Saricoban (2013) 36 students were expected to learn a set of vocabulary and motivation was the connecting factor between the two again (Özturan & Saricoban, 2013). In another study, students who used mobile medium, including SMS text messaging, seemed to have a more positive and fruitful learning experience than those who did not (Özturan & Saricoban, 2013). Chinnery (2006) states that in his findings CALL devices generally are more used for learning, such as examples like Rosetta Stone being so common when compared to a medium like MALL (Bahrani, 2011).

MALL, Mobile Assisted Language Learning, is another new form of language acquisition as described by Bahrani (2011). Essentially similar to CALL, MALL is even closer to the dimensions in which this CIMCC application, now in its first phase of user trial, exists (T. Endo, personal communication, February 26, 2015; Bahrani, 2011; Özturan & Saricoban, 2013). The qualitative data obtained through interviews in Bahrani's 2011 study show that MALL is both beneficial to learning and to motivation to learn. Because so many students in this day of age have choose to have smart phones, it only makes sense to find a way to teach a language though this medium.

As a college student surrounded by peers and students, I find that it is almost common knowledge that most students have mobile phones and tablets (Chinnery, 2006). Yet not only does nearly every student have one, but most students possess smart phones which are application enabled (Özturan & Saricoban, 2013). As previously mentioned, Miromaa's software is specifically an application for smart phones (CIMCC, 2013; Miromaa, 2011). One of the many goals explained by team member (and former Sonoma State

University Alumni Tomio Endo) is to revitalize the language through this app and in hopes to reach every and any members of the Pomo language community (T. Endo, personal communication, February 26, 2015). How are all members of the community to be integrated through a mobile application? This study aims to find out why and how the integration of a smart phone application can help revitalize a language.

AN INTEGRATION

Languages are being learned throughout the globe through CALL devices, yet very few are as endangered as the seven main branches of Pomo (Chinnery, 2006). Focusing mainly on the Eastern Pomo, Southern Pomo, and Central Pomo languages, each have phonological, phonetic, lexical, semantic, and pragmatic differences (T. Endo, personal communication, February 26, 2015). As previously mentioned, CIMCC plans to use the software from Miromaa Aboriginal Language and Technology Center in Australia to create an application (CIMCC, 2013; Miromaa, 2011). Though I have not personally seen, tested, or learned much about the initial phases of the application, I can already envision the future it has ahead of itself. Using quantitative and qualitative data and working with the preexisting data from the CIMCC, I wish to find out what would make an application successful for teaching revitalizing the Pomo languages.

Due to time constraints, interviews were not yet successfully conducted by the time of this writing. Though I was able to meet with Tomio Endo multiple times at the CIMCC and speak to Pomo tribe members, no information as to their thoughts on the application was recorded. In the future I plan to continue this project with the help of the CIMCC in order to gain an even better understanding of the linguistic triumphs and issues with this new learning medium. Because fieldwork is an important aspect in any study involving the revitalization of a Native language, it is important to this study

(Ahlers, 2009). In the future I plan on conducting short interviews with participants involving the following questions;

- What experience do you have with Pomo languages?
- Which of the seven languages are you the most comfortable with?
- Which of the seven regions do you identify with?
- Where does your knowledge of the language come from?
- What is your experience with language learning?
- Did you take a language in school?
- How do you feel about classroom language learning?
- How do you feel about technological assisted language learning?
- Have you heard of Rosetta Stone or another online/app based language learning mediums?
- How do you feel about an application being made to help teach Native languages?
- Are you aware of the other examples in the United States involving applications to help revitalize Native languages?
- Do you think this new medium will be beneficial? Why or why not?

The knowledge obtained through these few questions will help both this study and also the CIMCC's Pomo language revitalization project because it is beneficial for them to know how their work affects the Native peoples (T. Endo, personal communication, February 26, 2015). As the goal of this study is to better understand language acquisition, it is clear that this medium is beneficial to learning.

CONCLUSIONS

Working both with language as well as Native American peoples make it so there are many precarious topics and experiences. Due to the history between the settlers and the Native Pomo as well as the history between anthropologists and Native peoples there are many logistical hoops to jump through in order to make this project, both my own and CIMCC's, a success. Many different research methods, such as interviewing, quantitative data analysis, description, transcription, and inscription will be all be used as methods in order to obtain linguistic data (Schensul & LeCompte, 2013, p.63-68). Because much of this project deals with a supervised internship with CIMCC, there is still a portion of this project that is unknown or yet to be decided. Once a meeting and work is set into place for the two Sonoma State students in involved with the project, more can be done to obtain data. From research as to the cultural past as well as the semantics and morphology of the language during the initial phases and a few observations form the data collected can be made.

With this new technologically advanced medium there is much room for improvement in language acquisition. From the two studies previously mentioned the key factor between both was motivation (Özturan & Saricoban, 2013; Zhang et al., 2014). Motivation to learn a language when it is not a common or universal tongue, as there are many different branches of Pomo languages, can be more difficult. Fortunately, the Pomo community and especially those who are involved in the project take pride in their languages (T. Endo, personal communication, February 26, 2015). Languages are going extinct around the world at an alarming rate and it is ideas such as those created by MIROMAA and the CIMCC that are helping to lessen that amount (CIMCC, 2013; Miromaa, 2011). In the future more research can be done to find out the differences between the languages and why it is difficult to combine many semantically and phonetically different languages or whether it is better to make one universal Pomo language or keep the individual languages. In the short amount of time I had to research this project more questions came forward than answers. I hope in the future to be able to further this study or hope another researcher finds this project to be as fruitful as I can envision it being. In conclusion, the Pomo languages are going through the process of being revitalized through a mobile application and the results have yet to be discovered in this example. However, this new medium for language revitalization looks to be beneficial to the members of the community and those who with to help revitalize and study the language.

REFERENCES

About Miromaa. (2011). Retrieved from
http://www.miromaa.org.au/miromaa.html

Ahlers, J. C. (2009). The many meanings of collaboration: Fieldwork
with the Elem Pomo. Language & Communication, 29, 230-
243.

Ahlers, J C. (2012). Two eights make sixteen beads: Historical and
contemporary ethnography in language revitalization.
International Journal of American Linguistics, 78(4), 533-555.

Bahrani, T. (2011). Mobile phones: Just a phone or a language learning
device? Canadian Research & Development Center of
Sciences and Cultures 244-248.

California Indian Museum and Culture Center (CIMCC) (2013).
Retrieved from http://cimcc.org/pomo-language-forum-at-
cimcc/

Chinnery, G. (2006). Emerging technologies going to the MALL:
mobile assisted language learning. Language Learning &
Technology, 10(1), 9-16. Retrieved from
http://www.llt.msu.edu/vol10num1/pdf/emerging.pdf

Dubin. M. (2010). Who we are, where we come from. News from
Native California, 24(2), 28-31..

Jacknis, I. (1996). Alfred Kroeber and the photographic representation
of California Indians. American Indian Culture & Research
Journal, 20(3), 15.

Loether, C. (2009). Language Revitalization and the Manipulation of
Language Ideologies. In P. Kroskrity & M. Field (Eds.),
Native American Ideologies (pp. 238-254). Tuscon, Arizona:
University of Arizona Press.

Norton, J. (2014). If the truth be told: Revising California history as a
moral objective. American Behavioral Scientist. 58(1), 83-96.

Özturan, T. & Saricoban, A. (2013). Vocabulary learning on move: An investigation of mobile assisted vocabulary learning effect over students success and attitude.

Rosetta Stone® - Learn a New Language. (n.d.). Retrieved from http://www.rosettastone.com/lp/ppc/sale/?cvosrc=ppc.google.r osettastone&matchtype=e&cvo_campaign=Branded&gclid=C NCS05fFjcUCFRSPfgodPTsAnQ

Schensul, J. J., & LeCompte, M. D. (2013). Essential ethnographic methods: A mixed methods approach (2nd ed.) Lanham, MD: AltaMira Press.

Tribal College Journal (2013). BCC develops Montana's first Native language app. Vol. 24(4)

Zhang, R., Liu, C, and Chen, L. (2014). Listening strategy use and influential factors in web-based computer assisted language learning. Journal of Computer Assisted Learning, 30(3), 207–219.

ENGLISH AND ITS EFFECTS ON GLOBAL MUSIC: SOCIETY THROUGH CODE-MIXING AND CULTURAL CHANGE

KATELYN KINDER

HUMAN DEVELOPMENT MAJOR

SONOMA STATE UNIVERSITY

ABSTRACT

Does the use of English in songs from different countries make students willing or intrigued to listen to music not in English, or in their own mother tongue? Based in an anthropological perspective, this paper examines the pragmatic effects of the English lyrics used, as well as pronunciation of that English, in music produced for a globalized market. While North America is often described as a mecca of all races and ethnicities, typically we see music sung in only the most common language: English. To gather data, I surveyed SSU students by showing them clips of English lyrics from popular foreign artists. The group that I will be using for my own research will have their own background in either music or in performing arts. The two elements that I used for the bulk of my data was personal interpretation and pronunciation. Understanding the pragmatic effects of language selection (including the use of multiple languages) in popular music provides insights into how why and how students engage in cross-linguistic musical experiences. Through the use of music, I believe people can become open to learning new cultures and can see the world through a new perspective.

Key Words: Language Ideology, Music, Culture, Foreign Languages, Pronunciation, Globalization, Code-Mixing, Code-Switching

INTRODUCTION

In America, we listen to a lot of different music. If we look on the charts of the top 100 songs, we can see songs ranging from hip-hop, to pop, to country, and rock. If we look closely at who is on the top charts, we can see that in all actuality most of the people that we label as "American" musicians are actually from a different country and not actually American. As America is a country of many cultures and the mixing of cultures, I would have thought that foreign music or different music would be more accepted as a whole because of this fact.

Music has always been a huge part in my life and as well as learning about different cultures and languages. Ever since a young age, I have always lived amongst different languages and cultures than mine. When I started college, I was given the opportunity to write a paper about a topic that interested me and that focused on the use of education and cultural acceptance. After being given this opportunity, I decided to research how "Music can bridge the Culture Gap" (Kinder, 2012). I did this study through the use of foreign language music being used to teach children about different cultures and how to be accepting of others. I was given once again the opportunity to write and conduct research again, but this time with the emphasis on linguistic forms. I decided to continue with the research that, I had done back in my freshman year.

When looking into what research I would like to do, I wanted to look into why English would be used in foreign music where English is not a commonly spoken language. This has always been a question of mine as being a fan of foreign language music myself. Is it for international acceptance or to be able to shed a spot light on a new type of music? Another question for this project is can the use of English in foreign language music help bridge the gap between different music genres and cultures?

PREVIOUS RESEARCH

When I first started my search for research, I wanted to do a comparison of Asian music and their use of different words and sentences of English in their lyrics compared to European countries and bands deciding to do all English lyric songs instead of songs in their native language. After searching, I couldn't find a lot of articles on why English was used instead of native languages in European countries, so I decided to focus on Asian music instead.

One of the first articles that gave me my first stepping stones into being able to come to a conclusion and see how many different things interconnect was an article by Andrew J. Moody (2006). Through this article, I learned of the three types of coding systems that I will be using within my analysis of data. The three types of coding's are code-mixing, code-switching, and code-ambiguous.

Code-mixing is where one language will dominate the song, usually the native language of the speaker and then they will add a couple of words from a different language; these words are usually borrowed words; which means these words may already be used or known in their home country and within their language system. Code-switching is where two or more languages will be sung throughout the song. This may make the song to sound as if it the song is split 50/50 with the different languages. Finally, Code-ambiguous is where there many a word in a song that either means the same in English as well as the singer's mother tongue or may mean something completely different in both languages.

WHY AND HOW ENGLISH IS USED IN FOREIGN LANGUAGE MUSIC?

In articles by Lee (2004) and etc., we were shown different ways in which English is placed into songs that are different than the coding schemes explained above (Moody and Matsumoto, 2003; Moody, 2006; Kim and Lo, 2012). All of these researchers find that English was used through forms of single words, sentences, as well as single word and multi-word switches or musical fillers. Examples of single words are baby, kiss, girl, boy or other simple English words. Musical fillers consisted of words like, oh, yeah, go, etc., added in-between other phrases in the singers' native language but are used to go along with the flow of the song.

In articles by Lee (2004); Moody and Matsumoto (2003);Moody (2001); Lo and Kim(2012),they all look into the reasons why people use English lyrics in their songs. They found that many singers use this for expressing their own personal identity and being self-motivating for other through their lyrics. This was also found through the breaking of gender stereotypes, changing traditions, empowerment and modernization.

Through many of the lyrics, we are able to see that many women used English lyrics to be able to express themselves in a way they could not in their own language. Through the use of English, artists were able to show a new type of modernity in their country and be able to show their country as a global country because of their use of English. Many females used English to be able to break away from traditional and gendered stereotypes that are set for them in their country. Through these new words women as well as men were able to show something new that has never been seen before in these countries through their music until the 1990s.

It wasn't until the 90s, that the use of English was used past the naming of groups which caused for the possibility of international fan bases and viewership to increase (Lee, 2006). Many of these songs are made not for the intention of international viewership but as the generations of technology has become so big, the possible pool of consumers has grown as well. So the use of English is now not only used for expression but also a gateway for others outside of the country to be able to listen and enjoy the music, while being able to connect to it with the little bits of lyrics they can understand.

METHODS

The participants in this study are students at SSU who have a background in music and preforming arts, who either preform or sing on a weekly or monthly basis. Some participants were chosen for their previous experience with foreign language and some were chosen for not having any or only some experience with music outside of the English language. The way that I will be collecting my data is like how LeCompte and Schensul (2010) described in their book "Designing & Conducting Ethnographic research". I will be using their methods of surveys and brief individual discussions or group discussions to retrieve my data. I decided to do this compared to doing interviews with people, because I wanted them to give me there honest opinion of the music that they are been shown. I also wanted to see and hear from the participants how they really felt about the music and if they would listen to it again? Through using surveys, I am able to get data that can help me compare and contrast what peoples background are compared to how they might of interpreted the music that they are shown.

RESULTS

When I first started this project, I wanted to look at if the use of English could be used to encourage or entice students into listening to a new type of music. When I think of music, I do not think of the language that it is sung in because I do not see music as something that has language barriers. In my opinion, you do not need to understand the language of the song to be able to enjoy and connect to the music. This being said some of the results from my study contrasts with my beliefs on this.

My second participant felt like she could not connect to the music, she explained to me why she feels like she cannot. She described it as "I feel like I can only relate to music in English or Spanish because I can understand it and the message that is being said". She also talked about how she somewhat could connect to the beat but need either more English or for the song to be in a language that she spoke to be more interested in it. This was also the same answer that my first participant gave me as well.

For my three other participants that I surveyed, they gave a completely different answer. These three participants explained how they all enjoyed the study and how they were very interested in foreign language music. From talking to them, I found that all of them have listened to or listen to music in a language that is different than English on a regular basis. One of the participants told me that she likes hearing chorus that have a different language because it makes her want to learn more. She explained

> "I really enjoy music that shares two different cultures. Whenever I hear a song with a chorus that is in another language, I am more intrigued with the song. I like it because it almost makes me feel like I can speak/sing that language too. It also makes me want to learn what they're saying, therefore learning about the language".

It has been interesting to see the differences these two different groups because both are on completely different sides. This has given me some great work to analysis.

When conducting this study, I changed a few things on a trial and error basis. When I did the survey on subject #1, I used three songs that were from Asian artist but the last song, the participant told me was very confusing. So when I survey subject #2, I picked a song with an American RnB vibe to it and to the participant it still was too easy and too similar to the other songs. So when I did my survey for the third time, I decided to use an artist that sings in English but that their background was very different than the rest of the clips that were shown. After adding this song in as the third song, I got a lot of better reviews on it and my last two participants actually told me they would like to listen to that artist again. I also believe I got better results on this song because the pronunciation of the English was much clearer and the lyrics made more sense compared to some of the other songs I had played previously.

The second song was the song that got a lot of mixed views. For the most part over half of the participants could understand the English and thought that it was fairly well pronounced, but when it came to picking the country that they believed the artist was from, they either picked the US or a country in Europe. This surprised me a lot because when I first heard the song myself I could tell that it was a Japanese Rock band. This also brings up the point that is made in Moody and Matsumoto (2003), which in Japanese when using English in their Japanese songs they in a way are said to become "Englishized" and make the song sound like a full English song. Englishized describes that the song and the lyrics will make it sound more culturally English and not Japanese. Japanese artists have had to change the way things are spoken in their native language to be able to blend together the two different codes. From this description, it makes sense why most of the participants choose an English speaking country for this song.

Overall, I found that 60% of the participants enjoyed the songs that had one of the coding systems in place compared to only listening to songs in English. The coding system that worked the best in this study was Code-switching because the participants could hear a large chunk of English around some words of a foreign language. The addition of foreign languages in the music was different but new and interesting to many of the participants. This fact was interesting to be because when I first thought of conducting this research, I was only going to play clips that were of full English by foreign artists but not play any of the foreign language parts of the song unless that participant ask to listen to it.

DISCUSSION

When looking at the data that I got, I can see correlations in my data that I was not expecting to get when planning out this study. When first starting, I thought the English lyrics would possibly be the gateway to students being more open to music done in a different language. From my actual results, English did not change or get really any reaction from the subjects. The use of English to the group that were not interested in the end, helped them to understand something but it still was not enough for them to be intrigued to listen to more. While the other group that was interested at the end, were more intrigued when the foreign language parts of the song came on. The people that enjoyed the different clips of music, they all were very open-minded to music in general and did not see music only as a possible language barrier, but as an opportunity to learn more. This reminded me a lot of how I came to listen to a lot of foreign language music, that the interest in learning about new cultures and understanding something new was intriguing in itself.

While looking into why people may not be accepting of a new type of music, I started to think back to my previous research. In my other paper, I spoke about how the use of foreign language music may cause a stir with people that encourage or are for an English only America. For the English only movement, they want for America to officially declare English as the official language of the US. If thinking from this point of view, it would make sense for people to be skeptical of listening music in a different language than they know because they want to understand it to be able to enjoy it.

A question I thought of after conducting this research, is how and why some people are more open minded to new cultures and languages? While someone who may be very accepting of everyone cannot be accepting to music in a language that is different than the ones they already know. That question could open up a whole new research project at another time.

CONCLUSION

"Music has no language. It's the music and how people can connect to our culture" (BBC News, 2011). This quote was spoken by the leader of the South Korean idol group 2NE1 and soon to be American solo artist Lee Charlin or also known as CL. This quote was what inspired me to start my research project back in my freshman year of college. From that paper almost 4 years ago, came this research that looks into the topic of why English is used in songs where English is not a main language in the country. As well as could the use of these English phrases be able to bridge the gap between music and the language barrier within music.

From the study that I have conducted, I have come to the preliminary conclusion that English is not, the be all end all for people to be able to start liking music that is not intentionally made for an English speaking audience. For people to be able to connect or listen to different music, they need more than just a few English words splayed here and there in a song. There needs to be something within the person for them to be intrigued by something new or something different and wanting them to learn about something that is different than the norm around them.

After doing this small study, I think about different way that this research could continue or be able to broaden and look more into how people accept music as a whole. If I could be able to continue with this research, I would like to be able to go into the communities of people that listen to types of foreign language music and ask them how and why they came into this community. Was it is because of your ethnic background, or because of peer pressure, or was it sheer curiosity? This study could also bring up many politics in the community as many of these communities have different stigmas for the different types of fans in that fandom as well as other fandoms in the overarching community.

Overall from this research, I have found out quite a lot that I had not known about the lyrics of music that I listen to quite often. Learning this has made me appreciate the music and the community that I am apart of even more. It takes a lot for a person to listen and like a culture or a type of music or TV show that is different from them. They may get weird looks and lots of questions as well as people looking down upon them, but in the end of the day language is just words and you don't necessarily need to understand those words to be able to connect to the bigger meaning that is being said.

REFERENCES

Kinder, K. (2012). "Music helping bridge the culture gap."

K-pop singer 'honored' at mtv awards. (2011, December 11). Retrieved April 13, 2015, from http://www.bbc.com/news/world-asia-16212073

LeCompte, M.D., & Schensul, J.J. (2010). Designing & conducting ethnographic research: An introduction. (2nd ed.) Lanham, MD. AltaMira Press.

Lee, J.S. (2004). Linguistic hybridization in k-pop: Discourse of self-assertion and resistance. World Englishes 23 No. 3

Lo, A., & Kim, J. C. (2012). "Linguistic competency and citizenship: Contrasting portraits of multilingualism in the South Korean popular media1." Journal of Sociolinguistics 16, no. 2: 255-276. *Communication & Mass Media Complete.*

Moody, A.J. (2001). J-pop English: or, how to write a Japanese pop song. Gengo Komyunikeeshon Kenkyuu [Language Communication Studies], 1 96-107.

Moody, A. J. (2006). "English in Japanese popular culture and j-pop music." World Englishes 25, no. 2: 209-222. *Humanities International Complete.*

Moody, A.J., & Matsumoto, Y. (2003). "Don't touch my moustache": Language blending and code ambiguation by two j-pop artists. Asian Englishes. 6, no. 1: 4-33

Monty, A. (2010). "Micro: global music made in j-pop?" Inter-Asia Cultural Studies 11, no. 1: 123-128. *Humanities International Complete.*

UNDOCUMENTED LATINO STUDENTS IN HIGHER EDUCATION

GRISELDA MADRIGAL LARA

CHICANO AND LATINO STUDIES MAJOR

SONOMA STATE UNIVERSITY

ABSTRACT

This project helps to understand the factors that enable undocumented Latino students to pursue higher education. By exploring both high school factors – teachers, counselors, administration and/or applied policies, and personal factors – parents, mentors, and community members that have encouraged their pursuit to attend college (2 or 4 year university). In particular, the project focuses on policies and legislation, economics, college affordability, participants' assimilation process such as age of migration, support systems (community support, institutional support, family), and self-motivation towards accessing higher education and completion. The findings are meant to add to the current literature on undocumented youth and higher education, in particular at small public predominately White non-research institutions, as well as to highlight the processes and factors that affect the college going decisions for undocumented youth is displayed by framing this under a life narrative method, and conducting two open-ended interviews with two Sonoma State students. Participants were recruited via the mailing list of the Extended Opportunity Program of Sonoma State University. Through a life narrative, participants had the opportunity to express their stories and put emphasis on important factors that had influence on their decision to attend college. Findings suggest that mentioned factors were significant in motivating the participants to attend college. The most important factor found was the students' desire to help their parents. It is also suggested that for a higher opportunity of socio-economic mobility a person needs a higher education.

Key Words: AB-540, DACA, Higher Education, Immigration Latinos

I am researching the factors that enable undocumented Latino students to attend college because I want to understand how they can achieve higher education with an undocumented status. Specifically, I want to know what helps undocumented students to succeed in high school and encourages them to apply to college. What are some of the policies that enable them to attend college? Once they are in college, who supports them financially and emotionally that encourages the student to do well in college so that they continue until graduation? Do the families of undocumented students support them either financially or emotionally in pursuing a higher education? Are there any programs that exclusively help undocumented students? Why do they decide to follow their dreams in attending college knowing that they are undocumented and might not get the same rights as other legal residents according to the United States policies?

I will now talk about some of the main arguments and ideas that I have encountered during my literature review of the factors that might enable undocumented Latino students to pursue higher education. The scholars in the field focus on factors that determine whether or not undocumented students pursue a college education. These are affordability, level of support from family, peers, and school personnel, and federal and state policies and legislation designed to help undocumented Latino students pursue higher education.

I am an undocumented student; my parents brought me here when I was eight years old. Growing up I was not aware of the significance of being an undocumented student. It was not until reaching high school that everything started to matter. My friends began to apply to colleges and scholarships. I, on the other hand had to be careful to only apply to scholarships that applied to people without citizenship. I was to make sure that I did not apply to FAFSA because if I did, I ran the risk of being deported. There were so many details I had to look out for in the process of transitioning from high school into higher education. I had a hard time figuring out the process and sometimes I questioned what made me decide to continue with the community college. I wonder if other undocumented students go through the same experiences and why they decided to continue.

We should care about this because there are many undocumented immigrants in this country and there are many undocumented children now that need to have the same opportunities as legal citizens. We live in a country of immigrants so are we helping our immigrants succeed? We should care because those students are the future workforces of this country. Many were brought here as children and the United States has become their only home; most have no desire to go back to their home country. It is important that undocumented students like any other receive the opportunity to pursue higher education in the United States.

I would like to help my reader understand the differences between the legal resident or citizen and the undocumented college student and experience when planning on attending or currently attending college. What do undocumented students hang on to in the process of attending college knowing that they are in the United States with an undocumented status? Then we will understand if the recent legal policies are helping more undocumented students to pursue higher education and how. I want to find out what factors enable unauthorized students to pursue a higher education. Whether it is policies that include affordability, family support, or self-motivation.

I will organize my findings as follows: policies and legislation that enables or prevents unauthorized students from attending college, college affordability, other factors in assimilating to the United States, such as age of migration, and support systems which includes community support, institutional support, and family and finally one's own motivation towards achieving higher education are discussed.

Policies and legislation in the United States regarding undocumented students play a role in determining whether undocumented students even consider whether or not to attend college. Policies that make it possible for undocumented students to pursue higher education are discussed in Edward D. Vargas' article "In-State Tuition Policies for Undocumented Youth." The author summarizes some of the many factors that legislators take in consideration while making policies. Some of the factors include demographics, which explain why some states pass or ban political legislation to enable or disable unauthorized students to study with in-state tuition. Other scholars discuss policies that hinder undocumented students from attending college. In "Americans by Heart: Undocumented Latino Students and the Promise of Higher Education" Nunez, AM, and V. Sansone explain why unauthorized students get involved in civic or academics. Getting involved gives them a sense of belonging to the whole society. Children and young adults are brought here by their parents and through no fault of their own they are still criminalized and said to be a drain of resources. They face challenges created by policies that hurt them educationally, and in their economic mobility. The 1994 North American Free Trade Agreement (NAFTA) for example caused many economic disparities in Mexico. Many crop growers were unable to compete with the prizes of the United States. That resulted of many families not having the choice but to migrate north and establish their family. They discuss the limited access to financial aid, minimal social services, and little opportunity to find a good job. The author concludes that undocumented Latino students do act and behave as citizens and should therefore be treated as such. In the article "Undocumented Students' Access to College: The American Dream Denied" Chavez, Maria Lucia, Mayra Soriano, and Paz Oliverez explain the obstacles that low-income and undocumented students go through. Many low-income, undocumented students are the first in their families to attend college and that leaves them depending on the school to prepare and guide them for higher education. Most of them attend schools that poorly prepare them and their parents are unaware of how the educational system works and cannot help them. Many Latino students are not going into higher education; for example, the US Census indicated in 2000 that for every 100 Latino/a students that enter elementary school, 46 will graduate from high school, eight will go on to earn a Bachelor's degree, two will earn a graduate or professional degree and less than one will earn a doctorate (Chavez et. al 2007). The situation shows how an average Latino student has low chances of getting to college, but the outcome is worse for the undocumented Latino student. The Illegal Immigration Reform & Immigrant Responsibility Act, enacted into law by President Clinton in 1996, placed severe restrictions on undocumented immigrants' access to public and economic benefits, which included access to financial aid. That law made it very difficult to afford college. Then Assembly Bill 540 came into effect in 2002 and it allowed every student to pay in-state tuition regardless of his or her status. In 2006 Arnold Schwarzenegger vetoed Senate Bill 160, the California Dream Act that would have allowed students to apply to state financial aid (Chavez, et al, 2007). Through advocacy, organizing and researching they have made some changes in the institutional systems.

In "Undocumented Childhood Immigrants, Dream Act and Deferred Action for Childhood arrivals in the USA" Carol L. Schmid explains how undocumented children in the USA and how policies affect them. She gives an in-depth analysis of Dream Act and Deferred Action. Undocumented immigrants' rights are contested rights in the United States. Their status is at mercy of state and federal administration policies. In the article "Learning to Be Illegal: Undocumented Youth and Shifting Legal Contexts in the Transition to Adulthood," the author Roberto Gonzales, goes over the problems that come with the coming of age and graduating from high school. That includes going from inclusion to learning exclusion in the real world. That means students get a free education from kindergarten through twelve grades without being asked anything about their immigration status but then as they become young adults everything changes and they face obstacles such as policies that hinder them from obtaining higher education.

Other scholars discuss college affordability as a determining factor. In "Social Identity, and the Mobilization of Law: The Effects of Assembly Bill 540 on Undocumented Students in California," Leisy Abrego explains how AB-540 allieviated students' stigma. It also empowered them to pursue higher education. AB-540 helped students with their tuition but it was not enough, mostly only community college was reachable without financial aid at that time (Leisy, 2008). Michael A Olivas, in his review of "Undocumented Immigrants and Higher Education: Si Se Puede" (Review) goes over the legality of financial aid and the scholarships restrictions. The writer goes over some of the issues with scholarships restricting the money from going to unauthorized students but does not talk about Hispanic Scholarship Fund which for many years was restricted to United States citizens. Institutional support for undocumented students: including the role of community colleges, advisors, and their civic involvement. Rene Galindo, in the article "Undocumented & Unafraid: The DREAM Act 5 and the Public Disclosure of Undocumented Status as a Political Act," examines the first case of civil disobedience a group of undocumented students called DREAM Act 5. He talks about the civil involvement of students who take part in the community to make favorable changes. H Nienhusser, in the "Role of Community Colleges in the Implementation of Postsecondary Education Enrollment Policies for Undocumented Students," examines the case of City University of New York and their work for making their two colleges a welcoming place for undocumented students. The community colleges can be seen as a pathway to a four-year institution. Seif Hinda, in the article "Wise Up!" Undocumented Latino Youth, Mexican-American Legislators, and the Struggle for Higher Education Access," goes over the fight for AB-540 (in-state tuition). Those were students themselves getting involved to better the situation for every undocumented student. The authors Lyons Patricia, Lauren Coursey, and Jared Kenworthy, in the article "National Identity and Group Narcissism as Predictors of Intergroup Attitudes Toward Undocumented Latino Immigrants in the United States," explain the predictors that determine the attitudes toward undocumented Latinos as a whole. Studies show that most people are supportive towards undocumented Latino students.

There are other factors involved with undocumented students' assimilation to the United States that are important for the kind of involvement they take. Arbona, Consuelo, Norma Olvera, Nestor Rodriguez, Jacqueline Hagan, Adriana Linares, and Margit Wiesner, in the article "Acculturative Stress Among Documented and Undocumented Latino Immigrants in the United States," the study they did finds the differences between documented and undocumented students regarding separation of family, language and level of traditionalism. Abrego, Leisy J. in the article "Legal Consciousness of Undocumented Latinos: Fear and Stigma as Barriers to Claims-Making for First- and 1.5-Generation Immigrants," explains with interviews, that immigration is experienced differently depending on the age migration. It compares and contrasts 1st generation and 1.5th generation of undocumented Latinos' consciousness of their status.

Motivation for achieving a higher education: including personal motivation, support from family and the social networks. Nate Easley, Margarita Bianco, Nancy Leech, in "Ganas: A Qualitative Study Examining Mexican Heritage Students' Motivation to Succeed in Higher Education" the author talks about the desire to succeed in academics in order to honor their parents struggle to give them a better life. Perez, William, Roberta Espinoza, Karina Ramos, Heidi Coronado, and Richard Cortes, in "Academic Resilience Among Undocumented Latino Students," the authors explain that undocumented students with supportive parents, friends and participation in schools have higher academic success.

If the dominant theories about the factors enabling undocumented students to pursue higher education are that government policies, affordability, and the motivation that students have coming from their parents and peers that support them emotionally, then we must conclude that support from parents and peers is the one most suited to answer my research question as it is the only one that claims that family support is key towards unauthorized students pursuing a higher education.

THEORY

Critical Race Theory says racism is ordinary and difficult to address because it is not acknowledged. Interest convergence and material determinism provides an incentive for dominant racial groups to maintain existing social structures. Racism is socially constructed and, therefore, perpetuated through everyday behaviors and existing institutions. There are forms of subordination to undocumented students while in college because of race, language, socioeconomic background, and gender and immigration status.

Hallmark Critical Race Theory Themes are interest convergence, material determinism, and racial realism: Racism is a means by which society allocates privilege and status. Today there is a right-wing backlash towards an immigration reform. Now policies that involve certain immigration status are aiming to stratify people. The fact that undocumented Latino cannot apply to certain programs or scholarships puts them behind in their academics.

There is meso-level discrimination by Organizations and school institutions in my research. My participants suffered from meso-level discrimination from the school system. They both were rejected from participating in a school program. In the case of the first participant, she was rejected from receiving help from the Learning Center on campus. The male participant was rejected from receiving help from the Multi-Language Program. He said, "I still can't get in because of not being born here. Even though I am paying taxes and I'm like spending money and helping the economy I still can't benefit of that." Those programs are supplemental, they were made to help students in their academics but because they are federally funded they cannot join them. Another way in which my second participant was suffering meso-level discrimination was along his elementary career where he said he was just put aside.

In the micro-level, the second participant was the one that spoke more of his daily experiences with his white peers. He said, "They would try to avoid you every way possible because they always see you less than them." Throughout high school he was only fitting in with Mexicans and gangsters. Other than that, he was really ignored and felt less with the attitudes of his white peers.

METHODOLOGY

I used life narratives with my participants. Life narratives are life stories told by research subjects, or participants (Garner, 311). They can be like the unstructured interviews because I am only giving the participants a broad question and they can go on about what they think of it. One of the participants was contacted by the Sonoma State's Extended Opportunity Program mailing list. She is a sophomore that emailed me back saying she was interested in participating. Another student texted me saying he had a friend who would gladly participate in the research project. It was a great way to do it because it gave my participants freedom to really go into depth of why they thought they were in college. It can also have a negative side to it since the participants might go off topic a lot.

This methodology was the best suited for my research

question because I wanted to know what factors came up more in their life narratives. I did my fieldwork in the Sonoma State Library patio. I had two participants, a female and a male who currently attend Sonoma State University. I contacted them through the Extended Opportunity Program mailing list and through other friends. They both agreed to meet with me voluntarily.

FINDINGS

My first participant was a female sophomore at Sonoma State University. She was fairly young and enthusiastic to share her experiences with me. She emigrated from El Salvador when she was nine years old. She said how hard it was because she did not know English but she had a good third grade teacher to ease the transition. She said, "I was luckily placed in school with majority of Latinos many of the teachers were bilingual so they were able to teach me one on one and stuff like that." To her it was an easier transition when she felt comfortable with the students around her. She had the same teachers in the same school since third grade into eighth grade. Then she went on to high school and she just knew she had to go to a four-year college so that she could leave home. She wanted to prove everyone that she could do it. She received AVID support in her junior year in high school and that class helped her for the two last years of high school. She said that about ten of her classmates were in the same situation as her and so they helped each other with the college applications. College applications are more difficult for undocumented students. "It was really complicated for us, like three times more complicated, we took the time to do a lot of research in what we needed to fill out for financial aid and scholarships and stuff like that, because our scholarships are special, like special requirements." There are issues that came with applying to college, not all scholarships are meant to be hand out to every student. As undocumented students, they need to make sure to not jeopardize their status in the United States. For example if an undocumented student was to apply for FAFSA, the most common financial aid amongst peers, then they risk deportation. Aside from the AVID program, the Huckleberry Youth program also helped her throughout her high school years. That program allowed her to receive SAT preparation, which improved her scores. Financially, 10,000 Degrees was able to help her pay for college dormitories. She was able to apply for the DREAM Act the same year it was enacted in 2013. DACA or Differed Action for Childhood Arrivals also made her eligible to work that year. That year was also the first year that EOP at Sonoma State accepted undocumented students so she applied and got into the program. She expressed her excitement when she remembered the year of 2013 because it really made her life a lot easier. She remembers applying to colleges and getting accepted, she wanted to go to Humboldt because she had gotten a tour there from part of the 10,000 Degrees Program and another one from the Huckleberry Youth Program. She got many tours from those programs including to South California. She took advantage of all those free opportunities because she knew she couldn't afford it on her own.

She knew that her family wanted her to go to college and she wanted to go too. "I didn't want to do what my mom is doing right now. I want to be able to support her." She has very clear goals of why she is going to school, she doesn't want her mother to keep working cleaning houses, she understands the struggle that it is.

Her freshman year, she wanted to explore the different opportunities that Sonoma State had to offer to her. She moved into the dormitories and she remembers her mother wanting to cry because she had never left home. Her relationship with her mother was not the best. She felt like her mother did not value her education, she only judged her for her personality. She had to go to school meetings alone. Her mother was unable to go to meetings because of work and she understood but she was still hurt by the lack of interest in her mother.

When she was in EOP and she saw all the leaders, she wanted to be a leader too. She said, "I wanna do it, I wanna make a difference and prove everyone wrong" and so she joined and became a leader. She is working as a Community Service Advisor at Sonoma State University. As a CSA she gets the benefits of living on campus, a meal plan, and a stipend. She was also involved by volunteering with JUMP, tutoring elementary students. She sees herself in a student she tutors and that makes her happy. She knows that she is a role model for the students and her younger siblings.

Although she is now eligible for more financial aid she is still not available for federally funded programs in school. She was ineligible to receive help from the Learning center on campus because she needed residency proof. She still does not qualify for California grants, or federally funded scholarships.

The male participant was very open in his opinions about why undocumented students pursue a higher education. His parents brought him to California when he was around two years old. They were from a working class background. He remembers that because his father was never around because he had two jobs. He ended up going to kindergarten in a school in East Los Angeles. "It was hard because there was too many white people and I just didn't fit in because I was one of the few Latinos, they would just put me aside." As he transitioned into elementary school in Redwood City nothing much changed. He would get into a lot of trouble and he would blame his sister because she ran away from home at a young age. A positive to that was that he became independent, as he couldn't rely on his sister and mom. By high school he began to get better grades but he was struggling about whether he wanted to hang out with gangs, or go to college. By the end of his sophomore year in high school his mother was diagnosed with ovarian cancer and he realized that he needed to switch his life around. He needed to get an education so he can help his parents and his future children. "In college is where you have all those connections that later on are gonna help you in you future," he said as he emotionally talked about the importance of attending college. During his senior year of high school he really wanted to attend college but couldn't due to his financial situation. Fortunately, his high school mentor was able to get him a benefactor that would help him pay for living. Now in college, making friends has been hard due to all the white students that already have their own cliques and are not welcoming or inclusionary. His support system has been a church club where other Latino students get together and get to know each other. He feels comfortable with them because they have common background and struggles.

He is a Dream Act and Deferred Action for Childhood Arrivals recipient, with that he is able to work and pay for college and his own expenses.

ANALYSIS

Both of my participants had economic hardships but they were determined to attend college. They are DACA, Dream Act and AB-540 students, which have helped them sustain themselves in college. They are eligible for some grants and loans but still do not fully qualify for everything like legal citizens. They both had mentors in high school, which eventually helped them get to the university and pay for it. I found that it takes one person in a students' life to change their attitude towards education.

They do struggle in the process of being in college, there is a stigma that comes along with being undocumented. Institutions like the school system keep reinforcing the stigma with the differentiation it makes between citizen and undocumented students.

CONCLUSION

The dominant theories about the factors enabling undocumented students to pursue higher education are that government policies, affordability, and the motivation that students have coming from their parents and peers support them emotionally. If this is true, then we must conclude that support from parents and peers is the one most suited to answer my research question, as it is the only one that claims that family support is key towards unauthorized students pursuing a higher education.

I found that all the factors are significant in motivating an undocumented Latino student to attend college. The main and most important one that came up most in my research was the desire to help their parents. They know the hard work they do and the suffering that they went through to be here in the United States. Separation of families happened in both for two reasons. In the first case, her mother had to come to work first and then she was able to bring her daughter. The second case, the male was missing his father because he worked so much. I definitely saw that they understood the struggle that it takes to be here in the United States. They both want to improve their families' lives and be role models for other students.

The next question we need to ask is what are the factors that help retain students in college when the majority of the students are white and they feel excluded? The feeling of worthless than the white people came up with the second participant and it made me wonder. Some of the answers to that question would be the same for him, his mother's illness and helping is a priority. What about other students? What keeps them in school, documented or not?

We need to keep asking and doing research in students of low socioeconomic status so with that information we are able to help them and get more Latino students into higher education.

REFERENCES

Abrego, Leisy J. 2011. Legal Consciousness of Undocumented
    Latinos: Fear and Stigma as Barriers to Claims-Making for
    First- and 1.5-Generation Immigrants. *Law &Amp; Society
    Review*. 45, no. 2: 337-369.

Abrego, Leisy. 2008. Legitimacy, Social Identity, and the
    Mobilization of Law: The Effects of Assembly Bill 540 on
    undocumented Students in California. Law & Social Inquiry.
    33, no. 3: 709-734.

Arbona, Consuelo, Norma Olvera, Nestor Rodriguez, Jacqueline
    Hagan, Adriana Linares, and Margit Wiesner. 2010.
    Acculturative Stress Among Documented and Undocumented
    Latino Immigrants in the United States. Hispanic Journal of
    Behavioral Sciences. 32, no. 3: 362-384.

Chavez, Maria Lucia, Mayra Soriano, and Paz Oliverez. 2007.
    Undocumented Students' Access   to College: The
    American Dream Denied. Latino Studies. 5, no. 2: 254-263.

Easley, Nate, Margarita Bianco, and Nancy Leech. 2012. Ganas: A
    Qualitative Study Examining Mexican Heritage Students'
    Motivation to Succeed in Higher Education. Journal of
    Hispanic Higher Education. 11, no. 2: 164-178.

Galindo, René. 2012. Undocumented & Unafraid: The DREAM Act 5
    and the Public Disclosure of Undocumented Status as a
    Political Act. The Urban Review. 44, no. 5: 589-611.

Gonzales, Roberto. 2011. Learning to Be Illegal: Undocumented
    Youth and Shifting Legal Contexts in the Transition to
    Adulthood. American Sociological Review. 76, no. 4: 602-
    619.

Lyons, Patricia, Lauren Coursey, and Jared Kenworthy. 2013. National Identity and Group Narcissism as Predictors of Intergroup Attitudes Toward Undocumented Latino Immigrants in the United States. Hispanic Journal of Behavioral Sciences. 35, no. 3: 323-335.

Nienhusser, H. 2014. Role of Community Colleges in the Implementation of Postsecondary   Education Enrollment Policies for Undocumented Students. Community College Review. 42, no. 1: 3-22.

Nunez, AM, and V Sansone. 2013. Americans by Heart: Undocumented Latino Students and the Promise of Higher Education. Review of Higher Education. 37, no. 1: 124-126.

Olivas, Michael. 2010. Undocumented Immigrants and Higher Education: Si Se Puede (Review). The Review of Higher Education. 33, no. 2: 296-297.

Perez, William, Roberta Espinoza, Karina Ramos, Heidi Coronado, and Richard Cortes. 2009. Academic Resilience Among Undocumented Latino Students. Hispanic Journal of Behavioral Sciences. 31, no. 2: 149-181.

Schmid, Carol. 2013. Undocumented Childhood Immigrants, the Dream Act and Deferred Action for Childhood Arrivals in the USA. International Journal of Sociology and Social Policy. 33, no. 11/12: 693-707.

Seif, Hinda. 2004. "Wise Up!" Undocumented Latino Youth, Mexican-American Legislators, and the Struggle for Higher Education Access. Latino Studies. 2, no. 2: 210-230.

Vargas, Edward D. 2011. In-State Tuition Policies for Undocumented Youth. *Harvard Journal of Hispanic Policy*. 23: 43-58.

DOING & UNDOING MICRO-AGGRESSIONS: POWER AND PRIVILEGE IN DAY-TO-DAY CAMPUS COMMUNICATIONS

NANETTE REYES CRUZ

ANTHROPOLOGY MAJOR

SONOMA STATE UNIVERSITY

ABSTRACT

This study explores the discourse surrounding and within micro-aggressions at Sonoma State University. Simply put, a *micro-aggression* is a verbal or nonverbal discriminatory interaction involving, but not limited to, a person's ethnicity, gender, sexuality, religion, disability, or marginalized identity. Most SSU students have undoubtedly participated in, experienced, or observed a micro-aggression. On a college campus such as Sonoma State University, where there are visible majorities within the student population, micro-aggressions are a daily occurrence. Despite this regularity, many Sonoma State students find themselves struggling to identify or define micro-aggressions in the context of their own lives. Due to the lack of teaching of what discrimination (as distinct from hate crimes), students experience a cycle of systematic and internal oppression, which in turn leads to negative emotions and experiences running rampant within the campus community. This study focuses on spaces and trends specific to Sonoma State that reflect possible methods to combat micro-aggressions, as well as introduces a new paradigm in the study of micro-aggressions on college campuses. This is established through the use of several rounds of interviews, surveys, and ethnographic participant observation sessions that are modified for the study as more data are received and analyzed.

Key Words: Micro-aggressions; College Students; Discrimination; Marginalization; Language; Diversity

INTRODUCTION

As American society evolves in light of injustices and the beliefs of its people, there has been a switch in how discrimination is experienced. Since the outlawing of overt acts of discriminations and hate crimes, or *macroaggressions*, a phenomenon called *microaggressions* has become a common way a person experiences discrimination. Microaggressions, as can be deduced from the term itself, are small acts of aggressions that are commonly verbal or nonverbal forms of discrimination based on race, ethnicity, sexuality, gender, disability, religion, or any other marginalized shared identity. My research looks at those small acts of aggressions in an effort to learn how do microaggressions occur linguistically on the Sonoma State University campus. Some microaggressions are as simple as a person referring to another by a stereotype, for example: a student walks up to a friend of theirs and starts a conversation about their grade in a challenging math class, the first friend says "The only reason you're passing is because you're Asian, huh?" Microaggressions such as the given example occur daily in many classes regardless of subject matter and at times more often because of the subject matter (Boysen, 2012). Regardless of form, microaggressions have been proven to negatively affect students in the long run. The students who are affected generally experience microaggressions frequently or as a daily occurrence, a trend that appears in much of the research around microaggressions as well as in my own research. In conducting my research on the language around microaggressions, I was able to see a glimpse of how Sonoma students interact on campus-- particularly in classes and in public-private spaces such as bathrooms, and see how many students are actually unaware of what a microaggression is and how their words or actions affect their peers. This research lead to my findings of several possible ways and starting points for students to learn about microaggressions and discrimination in general.

THE PSYCHOLOGICAL CARE AND COPING OF MICROAGGRESSIONS

Within the last 20 years or so, research around microaggressions on college campus has become much more prominent. However, the large majority of this research is from the perspective of a clinical psychologists, and has led to an enlightening— but also a specific view of what occurs in the aftermath of a microaggression. In spite of the noted existence of intersectional discrimination and the plethora of marginalized groups, the majority of researchers, including Solorzano, Ceja, and Yosso (2000) and McCabe (2009), focus on racially charged microaggressions. In fact, when referencing Sue et al.'s (2007) breakdown of microaggressions into microinsults, microassaults, and microinvalidations, Yosso, Smith, Ceja, and Solorzano (2009) describe and define these sub forms primarily within the context of race, with minor references to identity and to marginalized social status.

In conducting interviews, focus groups, and surveys, researchers were able, over long stretches of time, to see how students developed in their university environment away from their home culture. Many of the questions that appear in the long term psychological research about microaggressions involve how students react to microaggressions individually or in groups, as well as how students cope from the stress of their experiences with microaggressions. Additionally, some researchers, in particular Boysen and Minikel-Lacocque, focus their research on certain aspects of the aftermath and coping of microaggressions on campus. Boysen (2012) focuses on microaggressions that occur specifically in the classroom and how they change classroom dynamics or are escalated because of unfair classroom power hierarchies. Minikel-Lacocque (2013) focuses on both microaggressions on campus in general and on the discourse and education on microaggressions on campuses. In fact, Boysen's and Minikel-Lacocque's research influenced my own research on microaggression discourse and language use.

ESTABLISHING AN ETHNOGRAPHIC NARRATIVE

While I decided to continue with the trend of conducting research on microaggressions through interviews, surveys, and focus groups, I also chose to utilize ethnographic participant observation, "…a process of learning through exposure to or the involvement in the day-to-day or routine activities of participants in the research setting (Schensul, Schensul, and LeCompte 1999)", and, as a result, received data that were unexpected and highly informative. Several of my interactions with other students and groups of students would involve me discussing my research and actually using the word microaggressions, and other times I would discuss my research without explicitly using the word microaggressions. These students were often friends and classmates, or fellow students who I met through the Sonoma State Hub who are involved with some of the cultural programs offered to the campus. The two students that I interviewed were both also involved with the Sonoma State Hub, and were aware of microaggressions prior to the actual interview. My anonymous survey participants were students who found my survey from my online postings on my personal Facebook page, or on my postings on the Sonoma State Hub's page. While the time period of my research was roughly only a few months, I was able to receive plenty of interesting data that will allow me to pose a larger and more complex research question for the coming academic year. The narratives I have heard and the stories I have read have helped to established a starting point on what about microaggressions that Sonoma State in particular, needs to begin focusing its efforts on.

"THE WORD 'MICROAGGRESSION' IS SILLY"

While the majority of my research was done through ethnographic participant observation, it was one survey response in particular that help to re-evaluate a significant part of my data. When participants were asked what they classified subtle forms of discriminations as, one anonymous participant respond with "I think the word 'Microaggression' is silly" (Survey Participant 8). It was this statement that suggested to me that it was possible that people are not sure how to talk about microaggressions, or simply do not want to talk about microaggressions. When reviewing my experiences as an ethnographic participant I realized that when I described my research using the term microaggression, students would be less likely to interact with me generally because the word was too technical and unfamiliar. On the other hand, when I began to describe my research in way that used definitions and examples to explain microaggressions, several students would easily realize what I was researching, and would engage in a conversation with me about the subject or even tell me about microaggressions they have experienced. It was also through these broadening exchanges that I realized that the student who wrote, "I think the word 'Microaggression' is silly" possibly did not fully understand the concept of microaggressions. This realization was reinforced by one of their other responses in which they mention how they believe "if something can be categorized as 'microaggression' it is not worth serious consideration. Specifically because of the prefix 'micro' which basically means tiny" (Survey Participant 8). However, despite this statement and a few other statements, several other students were able to give detailed accounts of microaggressions they experienced.

CLASSROOMS AND BATHROOMS

One student that I interviewed, Interviewee 2, was able to give several examples of both verbal and nonverbal microaggressions due to the fact that she experiences microaggressions on a daily basis.

Notably, she as well as my other interviewee, discussed how most of the time the microaggressions were not fueled by a desire to be hurtful or rude, but were generally well intentioned or simply from a place of ignorance. This trend has shown to correlate with on-campus locations as well. It is in the classrooms and in the "public-private" space of the bathroom where microaggressions reportedly occur most often.

In classrooms where the immediate and obvious power is placed in the professor, it is the professor's actions that primarily define how often and in what manner microaggressions are going to occur. Professors generally set examples for students, and in a classroom setting where class topics can often be controversial, it is the manner in which the professor handles and reacts to the topic and to the students' reactions that sets up how students will continue to react to classroom material and to their peers (Boysen 2012). During a microaggression, if a professor chooses not to inform the class that the statement or gesture was unacceptable, then students will continue to commit microaggressions, possibly with increasing frequency. Interviewee 2 experienced this in most if not all of her classes, due to her wearing her hijab. She described often being subjected to pointing, staring, and whispering across the classroom, and that no professor interfered, which permitted the pointing, staring, and whispering to continue.

In bathrooms, both interviewees discussed experiencing microaggressions in the form of blatant staring. Interviewee 2, who has experienced microaggressions daily, multiple times a day, spoke about feeling uncomfortable due to not knowing if her personal space would be invaded, as it has been previously in a public bathroom. Interviewee 1, who identifies as a transman (a man who was biologically assigned female at birth), spoke about how he would feel uncomfortable with what other men would think while in the public restroom and how until the Student Center was built in 2013, the only gender neutral bathrooms would generally be across campus. These experiences lead me to look more closely at safe places versus unsafe places and counter-spaces, spaces created to challenge microaggressions (Solorzano et al., 2000). Classrooms and bathrooms have both been firmly described as unsafe places. Sonoma State students, who are aware of microaggressions and habitually attend diversity programs or clubs or are simply aware of the Sonoma State Hub, list the Sonoma State Hub as a safe place for them. Because the Sonoma State Hub provides a safe place for students, students who experience microaggressions have not created counter-spaces, but instead tend to create sub spaces connected to the prior existing safe space within the Sonoma State Hub.

INTERSPACE, INTERNET, AND ISSUES WITH ESSAYS AND EXPOSITIONS

Another type of unsafe space is public writing. In the main taxonomy of microaggressions there is the divide of verbal and nonverbal; public writing would be categorized as being between these two. This is because writing is nonverbal due to its lack of a spoken aspect, but is also considered verbal because of the definition of the word—"of, or relating to, or consisting of words," and due to the nature of public writings to be quoted aloud (Merriam-Webster'sonlinedictionary, n.d.). During my research it became evident that multiple students were mentioning reading microaggressions on the SSU Confessions page on Facebook, or in class where students were using out of date and racist phrasings in their essays and homework assignments, or even an incident in the *Sonoma Star* (A Nauseating Perspective 2015) where an author used the word 'colored' rather than the appropriate phrase, person(s) of color. This wording has since been changed due to protest from the campus club Black Scholars United. For whatever reason, none of the students I spoke with went into full detail about these incidents they have encountered or heard about, but most mentioned it existing.

Microaggressions occurring in public writings are new in the sense that people are recently understanding what written microaggressions look like. These experiences are stuck in an interspace currently, occupying a space somewhere between where they are still not considered to be microaggressions and are instead labeled *cyber-bullying* or *stereotyping*, and a space where they are fully recognized as being microaggressions.

DISCUSSION AND REFLECTION

My findings have both been expected and unexpected. Much of the general data fell in line with thins I read about in the previous research or matched my own experiences. However, there were several subtle nuances that I never expected to find myself learning about and realizing that had an affect on the students on campus, including myself. That said—I realize that in my research there was a degree of bias from myself, and that I may have been overly empathetic towards my interviewees and participants because I as well experience microaggressions. My empathy for people with whom I share experiences, and my desire to reveal that microaggressions are a serious interaction could have easily colored my research, risking becoming a close-minded crusade of social justice. I like to think that it did not, and that I was able to, if not begin from an open-mind, at least carry the project with an open-mind to the end, and being able to portray microaggressions and the people involved as they are, and not how I solely believe them to be. The process of receiving counter-intuitive data, no matter how small, contributed to opening my mind enough to realize that microaggressions as a concept is not as accessible to others as it was to me.

CONCLUSIONS

Microaggressions occur daily. They occur in class, in the bathroom, online and on countless other places on Sonoma State

Campus. The frequencies in which microaggressions occur do not match the number of student that can adequately explain a microaggression. All of my research, whether it has been examining the space where microaggressions occur, the discourse around microaggressions, or the linguistic types of microaggressions, has lead to the simple conclusion that Sonoma State does not have enough programs, classes, or events that teach what a microaggression is. Because of the gaping lack of knowledge of what microaggressions are, students continue to act and speak in a manner that is harmful to their peers and likely harmful to themselves. The spaces occupied by students who are aware of microaggressions are singular and strive to teach others on all manner of diversity and acceptance; however, a singular space cannot possibly cater to the entire population of students and their specific needs. Students who do not learn about microaggressions from their teachers or from their experiences may not want to take the time to educate themselves by entering into a safe space such as the Sonoma State Hub. Those students who never learn will continue to perpetrate or observe microaggressions, and will not know the effect of their words and actions and will not go on to educate others about microaggressions. At current, there are no required programs or class units that all students, faculty, and staff are required to take that would educate them on types of microaggressions and their causes and effects. This lack needlessly perpetrates the cycle of systemic and internal oppression of the student population and limit students into not knowing how to talk about microaggressions or why they should. Solutions to this problem can be as simple as providing incoming freshman with a short discussion or lesson on microaggressions. However, in order to have students ideally learn about microaggressions, students need to be continuously reminded and faced with this knowledge. This could be done through required online trainings, seminars, or through classes. In an English or journalism class, students should be required to learn the proper language to be respectful to all persons. In leadership classes, students should learn how to communicate with their peers and team members respectfully and without abusing their hierarchical granted powers. Even the smallest amount of research has allowed me to learn and see what can change on campus, in continuing this research people can learn what Sonoma State needs to learn, can learn what information needs to become accessible. Students who are privileged and who have never experienced microaggressions need to be taught that the reason they might not be able to fully relate to others is because they may be unknowingly perpetrating discrimination and harming their friends. Their privilege creates a wall that limits how students can communicate in their day-to-day lives. Knowledge cannot erase privilege, but it can help the privileged to empower the marginalized.

REFERENCES

A nauseating perspective. (2015, January 27). Retrieved April 29, 2015, from http://www.sonomastatestar.com/opinion/2015/1/27/a-nauseating-perspective

Boysen, G. A. (2012). Teacher and Student Perceptions of Microaggressions in College Classrooms. *College Teaching*, *60*(3), 122–129. doi:10.1080/87567555.2012.654831

McCabe, J. (2009). Racial and Gender Microaggressions on a Predominantly-White Campus: Experiences of Black, Latina/o and White Undergraduates. *Race, Gender & Class*, *16*(1/2), 133–151. doi:10.2307/41658864

Minikel-Lacocque, J. (2013). Racism, College, and the Power of Words: Racial Microaggressions Reconsidered. *American Educational Research Journal*, *50*(3), 432–465. doi:10.3102/0002831212468048

Schensul, S. L., Schensul, J. J., & LeCompte, M. D. (1999). *Essential Ethnographic Methods: Observations, Interviews, and Questionnaires*. Rowman Altamira.

Solorzano, D., Ceja, M., & Yosso, T. (2000). Critical Race Theory, Racial Microaggressions, and Campus Racial Climate: The Experiences of African American College Students. *The Journal of Negro Education*, *69*(1/2), 60–73. http://doi.org/10.2307/2696265

Verbal, n.d. In *Merriam-Webster.com,* Retrieved April 27, 2015, from http://www.merriam-webster.com/dictionary/verbal

Yosso, T., Smith, W., Ceja, M., & Solórzano, D. (2009). Critical Race Theory, Racial Microaggressions, and Campus Racial Climate for Latina/o Undergraduates. *Harvard Educational Review*, *79*(4), 659–691.

THE TOOLBOX: RESEARCHING DISCOURSE AROUND CONFLICT MANAGEMENT PARADIGMS

PAULINA CEJA

HUMAN DEVELOPMENT MAJOR

SONOMA STATE UNIVERSITY

ABSTRACT

This paper explores discourse around three paradigms expressed when implementing and teaching conflict management in educational and after school institutions In Northern California; (1) Do schools try to control the behavior? (2) Do they find it as a way for the child to learn? (3) Do they find it as a way to mediate a bigger social problem? We analyze the sociolinguistic norms and terms used by educators with young children in and around the teaching of conflict management. Socioeconomic and cultural factors affect models of how an individual may possibly deal with conflict creating a barrier between methods taught at home and at school. With the implementation of ethnography research will be collected through interviews and observations providing data that will be analytically analyzed. Numerous elementary schools in Sonoma County have implemented the "Tool Box" method (Collin, 2006) to teaching conflict management; field research along with ethnographic data reveal the impact this approach has had on the surrounding communities. These findings identify novel pedagogical approaches to teaching conflict management in local schools and the potential impact on conflict behaviors in the surrounding communities.

Key Words: Classroom interaction, Linguistic community, Multicultural classroom, Socio-cultural, Sociolinguistic

Research on early conflict management has been readily and recently surfacing in the anthropological world. There are many types of strategies implemented but this study focuses on an ethnographic and anthropological approach within three possible paradigms providing discourse around conflict management. (1) Do schools try to control the behavior? (2) Do they find it as a way for the child to learn? (3) Do they find it as a way to mediate a bigger social problem? Within the bodies of the research article they rely heavily on social factors as well as cultural communities bringing paradigms to conflict. This review will analyze the research based on methods, theoretical perspectives, and anthropological contributions to the topic of conflict management. The main goal of this review is to identify methodological and anthropological methods to collecting and understanding the data.

PREVIOUS FINDINGS AND METHODOLOGIES

Throughout the review of various research studies it has became very apparent that most of the research in this field is not only relatively new but also includes one, if not all paradigms, in its study. There are a few that weighed heavily on their attempt to mediate a bigger social problem. Coghlan (2000) discussed how an English classroom provides optimal grounds for one to teach conflict management. Although research on these programs that aim to teach social skills, is scant, early studies indicate some progress on violence prevention when such programs are implemented continuously. (Coghlan, 2000, p. 86). She found that violence prevention programs couldn't be conducted in isolation, as entities in themselves. To be effective they must be fully integrated into the students program of study. She studied the effect that violence protection play (RIPP) had on the students understanding of conflict and how to manage situations. She noted that role-playing participants reported significantly fewer violence related injuries developed more positive changes in self-esteem and used resources such as peer mediation at a higher rate than did non-participants. (Coghlan, 2000, p. 85) The findings in this study were relatively qualitative and there were no controls of any sort; this is where the research should go in order to provide a full perspective of how effective this method is. However this study does highlight that English classrooms provide a great environment for these said tactics, they provide a positive outcome for the participants and cohesion is needed among both teachers and students to function properly. One challenge Coghlan (2000) faced was the need for integration between both students and teachers. She found that if discourse surrounded their communication the method would be unsuccessful in mediating the bigger social problem. This directly coincides with what Sheridan et al. (2013) haves stated about cohesion amongst teachers and students in his experience teaching the SWEP to schools internationally.

Sheridan et al. (2013) searched out to effectively transition education programs from west to other countries while still remaining sensitive to their possible paradigms. Sheridan et al. conducted their research based on two essential data collecting methods (Schensul & LeCompte, 2013); surveys and interviews. This provided them with solely qualitative data and they later found room for bias when they considered that the socio-cultural background of Filipino descendants placed social acceptance higher than most other backgrounds, swaying people from answering honestly on surveys due to fear of social isolation. However, there were some major findings in their research applicable to my topic of study. First, teaching methodologies must be consistent with the preferred learning styles of students and their socio-cultural context; it is important for practitioners (and researchers) to immerse themselves in the culture and find out the teaching method that best fits those societal customs. For example, the Filipino customs were to be more group oriented so there was far more group integrated projects than there would have been in a western curriculum.

Faculty should approach the educational experience as an opportunity for both co-teaching and co-learning. This is where both articles agree with each other, it seems that connectedness is needed in order to have a successful implementation of the said method. However, there seems to be some discourse around the way teachers view these peacekeeping methods; one that Hockette (2012) witnessed first hand.

Studies (Stevahn et al., 2000) showed that most children can comprehend and learn conflict management skills as early as 6 years old. Stevahn et al.'s research on integrating curriculum in a kindergarten classroom is a study that I found most influential applicable to my own perspective research. Their study provided very detailed methods of analyzing the sociocultural influence seen in these young children. The study explores the effects of conflict managements in classroom, and examines the extent to which kindergarteners understand conflict and how they solve their conflicts on their own. Stevhan et al. took 80 children and disbursed them into experimental and control groups, the experimental group was taught 9 hours of conflict resolution and friendship while the control received 9 hours of conflict management each week for 4 weeks. They found a significant difference between knowledge and retention of the conflict procedure, willingness and ability to use the procedure in conflict situations, conceptual understanding of friendship. They also found that children act in two ways to resolve conflicts naturally (1) impulsive physical behavior to get what they want or to avoid harm, (2) unilateral actions based on control or appeasement of the other person. According to social psychologist if training is conducted appropriately, kindergarten children will be able to learn integrative negotiation procedures to resolve conflicts. (Stevahn et al., 2000, p.75) Their final findings were that none of the untrained children attempted to use negotiation to resolve conflicts that occurred during freeplay. What was most interesting about this study was that they based their research on the idea that kindergarteners did indeed have the cognitive capacity to process conflict. However, the authors conclude that if conflict management is not taught to children, they will develop unhealthily, and will be destructive not only to themselves but to the surrounding society as well (Stevhan et al., 2000, p.179). While perhaps surprising, this position did agree with Murray's (1998) research on shaping children's thinking so they learn to be nonviolent.

Murray's 1998 study conducted a study of violence among young children that included nearly 5,000 students (40% African-American, 40% Latino, 16% European American) for over 7 years. He found that children often learn violent behaviors as early as kindergarten, and that without intervention, the violence tends to persist and to escalate. By the time children are eight years old, violent habits are almost impossible to break, and intervention progress should behind as early as possible, which is consistent with the paradigm that children are young and do not know any better until they are taught to know better. Following this paradigm leads us to research behind the "Toolbox Project". (Collin, 2011).

The Tool Box aims to foster the development of resilience, emotional intelligence, and other positive behaviors and skills in k-6 students. In 2010, Dovetail conducted formative and pilot research on their k-3 curriculum during a 15-week implementation. The research focused on ToolBox potential to positively impact students, schools, and family/community. Designed their system around three overarching objectives (1) to improve resiliency skills and assets for children k-3, (2) improve school climate and connectivity with teachers and students, (3) improve links between school, home and community in efforts to support the children's positive social, emotional, and behavioral growth. They found that the ToolBox improved resiliency skills and elicited positive results. The teachers found it easy to integrate the method into their standing curriculum and 97% said they would teach it again. One problem with their research is that it needs to have more depth and more research with a control group in order to provide a more thorough perspective. According to public school records, after implementation disciplinary actions have dropped 15%. Filed accounts of confrontations and violence have dropped as well by 28%. 92% of teachers in the school district stated that they found the method very easy to implement and would do so again. The following chart shows the drop in violence after implementation of the toolbox method.

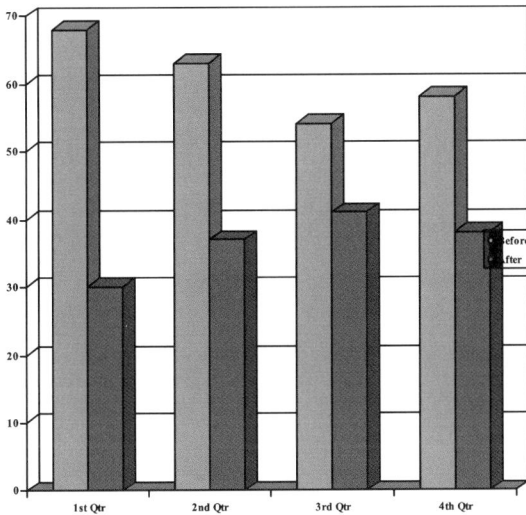

*Rates of violence during implementation
of the Toolbox method, based on Collins 2011.*

METHODOLOGY:
ETHNOGRAPHIC OBSERVATION AND INTERVIEWS

After IRB approval for studies involving human subjects, I began observation at an afterschool program Monday through Friday from 2p.m. to 4p.m. I observed a group of children on the asphalt playground, and in the classroom to establish a baseline of data. I was interested in finding out how many conflict altercations happen within a given day and how often these children work through the problems using the tools they were given or how often they revert to previous paradigms to conflict management. Five interviews were held amongst faculty members, team members of the afterschool program, and parents of the children to gain inside perspective on the effectiveness of the Toolbox method.

When implementing research methods the aim was to answer two key research questions: how does ethnographic documentation of explicit pedagogical methods to conflict management reveal effective implementation in a Sonoma County afterschool Program? What are the explicit and illicit procedures to teaching conflict management? Through extensive observation and data collection these two questions were answered.

PRELIMINARY FINDINGS

As a participant observer in the Boys and Girls Club afterschool program I have witnessed various encounters amongst children and documented their routes through conflict management. I have found that the Toolbox method is a widely accepted form of conflict management. I was able to sit in on a staff professional development session where one head faculty member taught the remaining faculty at the school how to correctly implement the Toolbox method. I later learned that this was to create consistency across the board for the children. In an interview with the principal it was revealed that the motivation for using this method is to create a stable and safe environment for the children. During field research I found that there is still room for improvement, and those teachers who have not been with the school as long are apparent by their lack of experience with the method. I witnessed an example interaction of how to incorrectly handle a conflict situation:

(Student A and B are playing Frisbee,
when Student C comes up and takes the toy.)

Student A: Hey! That's mine give it back!

Student C: No! Let me play!

Student A: You didn't ask and now I'm not going to let you now.

Student C: Fine! I'm taking the Frisbee

Student A: Give it back!

(Now running toward Student C and begins to physically hit)

Teacher 01: Hey! Stop it!

(She splits the students up and takes Student C away)

This situation would have provided a great opportunity to implement some of the Toolbox tools such as the: empathy tool, be kind tool, patience tool, sharing tool, and personal space tool, but the teacher is fairly new and assumed that Student C had started the altercation because that student had a history of fighting. Applying the steps to the Toolbox, it would have been revealed that Student C only wanted to play, and when faced with rejection not know to use the trashcan tool or patience tool, and instead simply took the toy, which is when Student A started the physical fighting. It is obvious that there is room for improvement, but this is only the second year that this method is being implemented into the schools, and progress, though slow, is being made. We can see examples of this in the interactions children have with each other without the supervision of a teacher:

Student B: Hey that wasn't very nice! That toy is mine.

Student E: I'm sorry I thought it was mine.

Student B: That's okay, I'll just put it in my trashcan tool.

Student E: Do you think we could share?

Student B: Sure.

This interaction reveals that Stud E took the toy of Stud B, but Stud B used the tools they were given and chose to not only use their trashcan tool but also their sharing tool. This was fascinating to see because it revealed that the children engage in the pedagogical conflict management methods being implemented in the school. This example showed the effectiveness the implementation is having in the school and on the children.

In relation to the three paradigms, observation revealed that the school fell within the second and third paradigms. (mediating a bigger social problem and seeing it as an opportunity to learn) During an interview with the schools principal it was stated that Mr. Jones (pseudonym) believed "the toolbox will hopefully help these kids later in life by giving them the tools to manage conflicts in an effective manor." This quote reveals how the faculty believes that this paradigm will help to solve the bigger social problem of violence in surrounding communities while taking this opportunity to learn and using it later in life. My preliminary findings seem to correlate with previous work in the field.

SIGNIFICANCE

As a staff member of the Boys and Girls Club, I found it very interesting to see how the teaching of conflict management has progressed over time. The implementation of the Toolbox method has just been introduced over the past two years to elementary schools in Sonoma County. If this study can reveal these methods to be beneficial, it could help promote implementation across the state. If correlation between this method and decline in violence rates in surrounding communities can be confirmed it would suggest new methods to conflict management that might decrease crime rates. The

Toolbox method is founded on the idea that teaching children how to effectively deal with conflict and supply the child with methods for managing conflict will allow the child to be successful later in life.

With what has happened recently in our surrounding communities, violence and shootings, I think that this paradigm could not have came at a better time. The significance of this study will be greatly increased if correlation can be found with surrounding crime rates. It not only will benefit violence in schools but also violence in communities, hopefully establishing a sense of safety in our towns. Conflict management is something a person will need to use all throughout life, whether it be in sports games, career fields, or everyday occurrences, it is important that children learn how to deal with conflict in a non violent way.

FUTURE STUDIES

It would be helpful to confirm whether or not these pedagogical methods correlate with surrounding crime rates within the communities? To add depth to the study, it would be important to reveal the children's perspectives on how they view these methods, as well as how the community views the methods of teaching conflict management. It would also be interesting to view how this method is used or not used in the individual homes of the children. Collin (2006) stated that without the cooperation of the teachers any method would fail, but I believe that without the cohesive cooperation of the teachers and parents any method would fail. Children are only in school for about six hours a day, some students go home, some stay in after school programs. In future studies the level of comprehension and repetitive use should be compared and contrasted amongst students who go home and those who say in the after school program where the methods taught in school are reinforced daily. Such future studies could incorporate group interviews with children and parents or teachers and parents, community questionnaires to view the perspective of such paradigms, individual child interviews to gain insight, and comparing of crime rates before and after implementation.

CONCLUSION

Though research on this topic is seemingly very young and only preliminary, some studies that have researched peace-keeping strategies or methods to conflict management have revealed that there is significance to teaching young children how to manage conflict properly. It is exciting to think about how my current research will be able to help the surrounding the communities. However, in my preliminary literature review on the topic, I could not find any comprehensive cross-cultural comparisons on culturally specific paradigms of conflict management. I am hopeful that my three will prove to be helpful in navigating my way around the field. This study has made it clear that there are definite advantages to teaching conflict management to young children, and it is also important for teachers and children to work as a cohesive entity. Lastly, it will surely prove to be difficult but there is room to research the impact that this conflict management has on the amount of violence the surrounding community is experiencing before and after integration of such methods.

REFERENCES

Collins, M. (2011). Tools for learning- tools for life. Dovetail Learning. WestEd, Health

Coghlan, R. (2000). The Teaching of Anti-Violence Strategies within the English Curriculum. The English Journal, 89, 78-127

Hockett, E. (2012). Developing a Peace and Conflict Resolution Curriculum for Quaker Secondary Schools in Kenya. Journal of Research on Christian Education, 72, 23-54. doi:-10.1080/10656219.2012.658603

LeCompte, M. D. & Schensul, J.J. (2010). Designing & Conducting Ethnographic Research: An Introduction. (2nd ed.). Lanham, MD: AltaMira Press.

Murray, B. (1998). Shaping children's thinking so they learn to be nonviolent. doi:-10.1080/10615479.1998.987456

Sheridan, M. J. (2013). Cultural Humility and Shared Learning as Hallmarks for International Teaching: the SWEP Experience. doi:-10.1080/02615479.2013.805190

Stevahn, L., Johnson, R., Oberle, K., & Wahl, L. (2000). Effects of Conflict Resolution Training Integrated into a Kindergarten Curriculum. Child Development. 71(3), 772-784. doi:-10.1080/09768954.2000.785983

TERRORISM IN THE MODERN WORLD:
THE CHANGING DEFINITION OF TERRORISM AND ITS IMPLICATIONS

MELISSA RITCHEY

ANTHROPOLOGY MAJOR

SONOMA STATE UNIVERSITY

ABSTRACT

This paper discusses the changing ideology, framing, and meanings of the word 'terrorism' in todays world. By colloquial definition, terrorism is the use of violence and intimidation in the pursuit of political aims (Asal, De La Calle, Findly, & Young, 2012) but ever since the 'terrorist' attacks on September 11, 2001, this term has changed to mean a multitude of different things. What has caused these changes, and what are the future implications for the usage of a word that holds such a strong cultural meaning? Overall, how have these nine letters turned into a term that can refer to a specific area in the world and those who come from it, a specific religious belief, and (but not limited to) those who attack the U.S. (and its interests)? The implications for this powerful word will be something the world must deal with for a long time and by distinguishing the different definitions of terrorism and their implicit and explicit consequences, possibly a better approach to future violence can occur.

Key Words: actor vs. action based approach, coded language, covert/tacit policy, globalized terrorism language ideology, terrorism, universal definition

Every day in the United States and other Western countries, a newscast about a terrorist attack or counter terrorism polices occurs. It seems like a day does not go by that there is not a new terrorist attack or discussions about the government not doing enough to fight the *War on Terror*. But what is terrorism and how does a word that can mean so many different things become so simplified that it is used to cover a multitude of different actions against the Western world, culture, and freedom? This paper will explain the numerous current definitions of terrorism in the United States that have been adopted by other Western cultures, analyze the difficulties in defining such a highly coded word, and the implications of these challenges. With a cultural and linguistic anthropological approach, the shift in the ideologies around terrorism that occurred after the September 11, 2001 attacks on Washington D.C. and New York, New York and the consequences of that shift will be discussed with an example from current uses of the word terrorism in media discourse.

There are several contemporary, academic ideologies around the definition of terrorism and terrorist organizations. There is an exceptional need for a useful operational definition that can be used and applied across all countries and social platforms. As Dingley (2010) discussed, it is hard to define every human act and behavior within the confines of legal terminology, so using terrorism to cover a wide range and general category of acts must suffice. There has been a multitude of attempts to narrow down this category and mark out the boundaries of what is considered a terrorist act and where to draw the line between terrorism and other types of violence. One of the more prominent and influential definitions is provided by the U.S. Department of State, in Title 22 of the United States code, Section 2656(d) (Ruby, 2008). Within this article, three vital criteria are given that separates terrorism from other sorts of violence. First, the act must be politically motivated for it to be considered a terrorist act. There must be some sort political agenda behind the violence in an attempt to change, influence, or guide a government policy. Second, the violence must be directed toward noncombatants. The intended victims are not members of military services or military members who are not directly involved in the violence and hostilities. To be terrorism, it must be directed towards civilians who are not prepared or able to defend themselves. The third requirement is that the group committing the violent acts is either sub-national (not a government or nation-state) and/or a clandestine agent (secretive or illicit). It is important to note that even though a nation-state attacks noncombatants, it is still not considered terrorism by this definition. Also, the victims of clandestine attacks do not know it is happening and that they are attacked unaware (Ruby, 2008). These three criteria must be met for a group or action to be considered terrorism. Without one of them, it fails to meet the mark, according to the U.S. Department of State.

There is a certain amount of grey area present among that definition that allows for the U.S. Government to claim terrorist attacks or to avoid labeling a certain act as terrorist in nature. For example, the U.S. bombing of Libya ended with the killings of thousands of civilians, but because the United States military was the entity involved in the killing, it is not considered a terrorist act (Ruby, 2008). This falls under the concealed implications of the policy, where the overt (or official) use is to define terrorist acts, but the covert implication is to keep the United States from being considered a terrorist group in its military actions oversees (Wiley, 2004). This has crossed over into the normal, mundane use of terrorism and the ideologies around it. Lippi-Green (2004) defined ideologies as a group of beliefs that surrounds everything in languages and cultures. There are many different ideologies surrounding terrorism in the United States and the way that the word is coded in American speech acts, also has very significant consequences. In a TEDx Talk (2013), López discusses coded symbols and terms in language and how these coded symbols are constantly used in politics. The term terrorism or terrorist holds enormous amounts of meanings and implications in Westernized culture since the September 11, 2001 attacks on Washington D.C. and New York. The term is inherently derogatory and whenever it is used, people use the coded language surrounding it to determine beliefs about the topic or violent act that may or may not be true (Asal et al., 2012)

In the literature world, another addition to this definition is generally considered. In addition to political agendas, sub nation, clandestine, and the targeting of noncombatants, an act that is intended to install terror and create a "fearful state of mind" (Ruby, 2008, p. 11) in a target audience (not necessarily the victims) is considered terrorism. Terrorism can also be seen as an act that is committed outside (or as an attack) on the rules of a society (Ruby, 2008). An act of terror ignores the laws and rules of war that separate military from civilian and flaunts them to bring the war and violence back amongst the people. It can be seen as an attack against society itself and the accepted rules of a society that dictate how people should act. This is why Americans and others in the Western world find terrorism so frightening and so senseless (Dingley, 2010).

Behind these criteria and the sociopolitical study of terrorism is a difficult challenge to create a universal, operational definition. Because the phrase terrorism has been used in the past to describe many different actions and is now used to refer to a particular type of violence, the methods behind determining this working definition must cover many different facets. First of all, it must be said that terrorism is seen through not only the victim's eye, but through the terrorist and the audience's point of view. Current definitions, like the ones discussed earlier, and discussions around terrorism tend to be analyzed and created only from a Western perspective (generally the victims or audience) based on post-Enlightenment ideas of war and violence, where war is defined as conflict between peoples represented by armies meeting on a battlefield with clear boundaries between the civil and military (Dingley, 2010). Without including non-western ideology, a skewed idea of what creates terrorism and what is consider a terrorist attack is made.

Different groups define terrorism in different ways and have different views on what is considered illegal or immoral. If an organization or government views terrorism as an act with no moral justification (in addition to other factors such as the ones listed above), they will have a different conception of terrorist attacks than a government who views terrorist acts based solely on political or territorial aspects. For instance, violence against noncombatants in the name of jihad (holy war) is viewed as not being a terrorist attack by some countries in the Middle East, Central Asia, and Northern Africa because it is morally justified. They simply are politically aimed attacks against the evils in the world-in this case Western capitalism and its excessiveness. In other situations, the term *freedom fighter* or *revolutionary* is used to describe perpetrators of violent attacks that may meet the U.S. Government's idea of terrorism but within the historical, social and cultural context of that region, the plight is morally justified and therefore not a terrorist action (Ruby, 2002). Observing and analyzing any factor of human action needs to be kept within its social, cultural, political, and/or historical context. This is a main theoretical component of anthropology, whether it be cultural relativity or historical particularism supported by Boas (1920). Taking the different ideologies around terrorism out of context and emphasizing only a Western view of the act limits the ability to decrease terrorist attacks and understanding.

There are two main approaches to defining terrorism, one being the action based approach and the other the actor based approach. They both have their benefits and disadvantages, but it is important to understand both to be able to get a complete understanding of how terrorism is used in daily discourse as well as in academia. The action based approach conceptualizes terrorism as an act of violence and measures each attack on the violence that ensues and declares it terrorist or not based on certain distinctions. The Global Terrorism Database (an action-based search engine of terrorist acts) sets the criteria for terrorism as the act must be intentional, violent, and committed by subnational perpetrators. It also must have at least two of the following: has a political, social, economic, or religious goal, occurs outside the context of legitimate warfare, and its intention is to send a message or point to large audience. Action based approaches view terrorism as a type of insurgency tactic and looks at different aspects of the attack while the actor based approach labels violence depending on if the insurgent group has territorial control of an area within a state's borders or not (Asal et al., 2012). This approach focuses on particular features of a violent group, such as whether they hold territory, operate underground, or have established trade networks. Scholars using an actor based approach view groups who have control of a territory as inherently not terrorist but once they step out of the boundaries of their control, they will result to terrorist actions. Therefore, groups without control of land tend to result to terrorism and only groups acting in areas not within their control can be considered terrorists (Asal et al., 2012). Depending on which approach is used, the definition of terrorism differs, and some violent acts are left out while others are included. This will then affect the cultural and social view of terrorism, especially when promoted by the media.

Now that the challenges around creating a definition of terrorism have been discussed, a more comprehensive look at the shift of ideologies around terrorism after the September 11, 2001 attacks on New York and Washington can be taken. Before these attacks, terrorism discourse tended to revolve around and reference individual groups working within countries against certain entities. After 9/11 and the declaration of the *War on Terror* by former president George

W. Bush, a Western (Americanized) ideology around terrorism evolved. This ideology put the focus on a globalized, international terrorism that involves extremely symbolic, clandestine and highly networked acts of aggression and violence. The term *globalized terrorism* itself assimilates many different kinds of violent, political and religious acts as it unifies and amplifies the threat into something bigger and more intense. When an attack is deemed terrorism, it becomes less about politics and more about a problem of security and *counter-terrorism* (Koshy, 2009). This can be seen when watching the newscasts following any terrorist attack (such as the Boston bombings or the rise of ISIS); first it begins as a serious violent act(s) with the listing of numbers of deaths and injuries, then the discourse turns to how can there be better protection and if the government (and president) is doing everything possible to support counterterrorism and further the war on terror.

The catalyst for this shift occurred when former president George W. Bush (2001) declared in his address to congress and the American people on September 20, 2001, "Either you are with us, or you are with the terrorists." He then goes on to declare that any government, regime, or peoples harboring or supporting terrorist groups will be considered hostile against the United States (Bush, 2001). This set the standard for the war on terrorism and created a binary ideology around a more complex issue which causes the use of terrorism or terrorist to describe entities that are not actually terrorist actions based criteria set up by the Department of State or academic scholars. There are many examples of people in the United States using the term terrorist or terrorism to describe actions or people who are not by any academic or legal definitions. This change in the use of terrorism reflects the changing ideology around terrorist acts and who commits them that began with the former president's declaration of a war on terrorism. Only one example will be used in this paper, but just by being more linguistically aware of the context that the term terrorism or terrorist is being used, a better understanding of the agenda and beliefs behind terrorism in the United States can be uncovered.

An instance where terrorism is used outside its legal definition occurs in an interview of the St. Louis leader of the traditionalist Ku Klux Klan (KKK) by MSNBC's Chris Hayes on November 12, 2014. This interview was in response to the KKK's declaration of war on the people (more specifically, the protestors) of the city of Ferguson, Missouri. Within the interview, a flyer being handed out by the KKK is discussed that threatens a backlash to those "terrorists masquerading as 'peaceful protestors' (Msnbc, 2014). The use of terrorist in this context is important to analyze as it is being used to describe a few of the activists involved in the Ferguson, Missouri protests of the failed indictment of the Darren Wilson, a police officer who killed Michael Brown. In addition, the comments made by viewers on the youtube.com page include a variety of examples of the different ideologies and beliefs around terrorism that exist in the Western world.

The leader of this chapter of the KKK, and presumably involved in the creation of the pamphlet, seems to view the protestors in Ferguson, Missouri as terrorists, and therefore (in the KKK's view) should be treated as such. He (and the KKK) use Missouri State law and United States law to defend their claims of protection and evoke the "you are with us, or you are with the terrorists" ideology adopted by the Bush (2001) administration. The very act of claiming these protestors are 'terrorists' based on their alleged threats towards whites in the St. Louis area goes directly against the legal definition of the word given by the U.S. Department of State and other definitions. One, because it was a threat, the attack (if it were to happen) would not be clandestine. Two, these possible actions would not be political, religious, etc. In this instance, using the term 'terrorist' caused different implications and affects towards the target audience and is playing on the American fear of terrorism. People are continually using language to communicate with the world and to affect those around them, and the use of terrorism in this speech act is definitely a very prominent and dangerous example of this (Bailey, 2004).

Analyzing the comments on youtube.com videos or any embedded video on the internet allows for an almost ethnographic type of environment, as it gives us the ability to see how different people use language to affect those around them. Often there is a hidden agenda behind the uses of terrorism, as shown in the video analyses, but other times there is just the unconscious use of the term that shows exactly what the general public's ideologies are around terrorism in the Western world. One of the comments of the Msnbc (2014) video that brings to light another important (and troubling) aspect of American terrorism ideology: the connection between Islam and terrorism. User dominicandiva777 (Msnbc, 2014) stated: "When violence is committed by brown skinned people it is labelled as 'terrorism'. (blacks, middle easterners, Asians, Hispanics). When it is committed against brown skilled people it is labelled as 'keeping the community safe'…" This user is bringing to light a common ideology that terrorism is only committed by non-white, non-western, people, especially those of the Islamic faith, generally from the Middle East or Northern Africa. Another comment also focuses on this aspect of terrorism ideology as well. Steve Abalon (Msnbc 2014) stated "All who believe in Islam are terrorist[s], one must only read the Koran to know that…" This user is directly and consciously linking terrorism to Muslims and therefore is saying that all Muslims are terrorists, no matter their denomination or where they live. This is a more extreme case involving linking Islam to terrorism, but it does show the common ideology in the United States and other Western cultures that Islam is an inherently terrorist, violent religion that must be exterminated to defend Western culture and freedom (Mamdani, 2005).

The use of terrorism in today's world offers some troubling examples of how Western culture views itself and others (prominently, Middle Eastern Muslims). The US Department of State's definition only provides a limited delineation of terrorist acts and causes many covert implications in the mundane, colloquial use of the word. There are many difficulties in defining terrorism, including the need to always be aware if someone is using an action based approach or an actor based approach, so as to know which way the information is bias. The heavy coding around terrorism and the shift in the ideologies around it in the United States seems to have been caused by the September 11, 2001 attack on Washington D.C. and New York, and the proceeding speech by the former president George W. Bush. Declaring a war on terrorism and creating the binary, 'us' (the free, Christian world) or 'them' (the terrorist, Islamic world) ideology has caused a distorted use of the word terrorism in everyday speech as exemplified by the MSNBC interview of the leader of the KKK. There is a need for more people to be aware of the coded language behind terrorism and the hidden agendas behind its use in American speech acts. With more anthropological analyses of the word, hopefully a better, universal definition can be made, and the derogatory implications of its use can be removed from being synonymous with Islam.

REFERENCES

Asal, V., De La Calle, L., Findly, M., & Young, J. (2012). Killing Civilians or Holding Territory? How to think about terrorism. *International Studies Review, 14(3)*, 475-497.

Bailey, R.W. (2004). American English: its origins and history. In E. Finegan & J.

Rickford (Eds.*), Language in the USA: Themes for the Twenty-First Century*. (pp. 3-17). Cambridge: Cambridge University Press.

Boas, F. (1920). The Methods of Ethnology. *American Anthropologist, 22(4),* 311-321.

Bush, G. W. (2001, September 20). Address to a Joint Session of Congress and the American People. The White House. http://georgewbush-whitehouse.archives.gov/news/releases/2001/09/20010920-8.html

Dingley, J. (2010). *Terrorism and the Politics of Social Change: a Durkheimian Analysis*. Farnham, Surrey: Ashgate Publishers.

Duranti, A. (1994). *From Grammar to Politics: Linguistic Anthropology in a Western Somoan Village.* Berkeley, CA: University of California Press.

Msnbc. (2014, November 12). *KKK Is Ready For 'War' In Ferguson | Msnbc.* Retrieved

from https://www.youtube.com/watch?v=MP8Of6gbZaM

Koshy, N. (2009). Revisiting the terrorism discourse. *Economic and Political Weekly*, 44(26/27), 44-46.

Lippi-Green, R. (2004).   Language ideology and language prejudice. In E. Finegan & J. Rickford (Eds.*), Language in the USA: Themes for the Twenty-First Century*. (pp. 289-304). Cambridge: Cambridge University Press.

TEDx Talks. (2013, March 8). *Dog Whistle Politics: Ian Haney Lopez at TEDxUOregon*. Retrieved from https://www.youtube.com/watch?v=qibFwUNDZX4

Mamdani, M. (2005). *Good Muslim, Bad Muslim: America, the Cold War, and the roots of terror.* New York: Random House.

Ruby, C. L. (2008). The definition of terrorism. *Analyses of Social Issues and Public Policy, 2(1),* 9-14.

Smith, L. (2014, September 26). "The Face of Terrorism?" [Web log comment]. Retrieved from http://thyblackman.com/2014/09/26/the-face-of-terrorism/.

Wiley, T. G. (2004). Language planning, language policy, and the English-Only Movement. In E. Finegan & J. Rickford (Eds.), *Language in the USA: Themes for the Twenty-First Century.* (pp. 319-338). Cambridge: Cambridge University Press.

NUCLEAR POWER DISCOURSE: WHY BODEGA BAY RESIDENTS NEEDED NUCLEAR POWER LIKE A HOLE IN THE HEAD

MELISSA MCLEES

ANTHROPOLOGY MAJOR

SONOMA STATE UNIVERSITY

ABSTRACT

This paper identifies elements of nuclear power rhetoric found in the historic Bodega Bay antinuclear power movement, and compares them to themes found in similar antinuclear movements and nuclear power disasters. The case study of the Bodega Bay Nuclear Power Plant, proposed in 1958 but never constructed, is central to interpreting the evolution of nuclear rhetoric. Residents of the small coastal community utilized a number of strategies to fight against Pacific Gas & Electric's nuclear ambitions. An analysis of satirical endeavors, newspaper articles, pamphlets, and music provides the history of the anti-nuclear movement. In comparison, the discourse around the fully commissioned and completed projects of the operational Diablo Canyon Power Plant and the decommissioned San Onofre Nuclear Generating Station are analyzed for similar patterns found in opposition to construction and commission. Discourse following the recent Fukushima Daiichi disaster in 2011 was predicated on the same warnings that prevented, decommissioned, or challenged the operation of the three California-based nuclear power centers, and sufficiently demonstrates the contemporary state of nuclear power rhetoric. Throughout each instance of antinuclear protest, successful or otherwise, the discourse reflects the correlation between public perception of nuclear power and identity.

Key Words: Nuclear Power Discourse, Anti-nuclear Movement, Discourse Analysis, Environmentalism, Activism

Prior to 1958, the rural fishing village of Bodega Bay, California, was essentially isolated from industrial influences and maintained a reputation as a quiet, tight-knit community. However, when Pacific Gas & Electric proposed the construction of a nuclear power facility along the Sonoma county coastline, Bodega Bay residents designed a passionate and innovative campaign to stop the development of their beloved Bodega Head peninsula, forever changing the rhetoric of nuclear power activism. PG&E was eventually thwarted by the efforts of the community, but not before breaking ground on the project, creating the "Hole in the Head" intended as the foundation of the facility. Nowadays, the "Hole in the Head" found on Bodega Head serves not only as a scar of nuclear development, but as a reminder to residents that words have the power to help people affect the world around them. While the rhetoric used in the Bodega Bay antinuclear movement has resonated with contemporary antinuclear activists, a shift in how words relating to identity and public opinion of nuclear power can be found by analyzing the antinuclear and pronuclear campaigns since 1958.

Initially, the argument of the Bodega Bay residents concerned the obstructed view of the small picturesque bay and adjacent Pacific Ocean. The State Division of Parks and Beaches intended to preserve scenic Bodega Head and surrounding areas prior to PG&E's proposal (Peterson, Hedgpeth, Neilands, Pesonen, and P.H.A., 1963, p. 139; Walker, 1990, p. 325; Wellock, 1992, p. 193). Due to the isolated nature of the town, residents were determined in their efforts to prevent the development of Bodega Head (Walker, 1990, p. 347). Some have even acknowledged this movement as the direct result of a postwar environmental era reflecting changing popular opinion about the nuclear industry (Walker, 1990, p. 347). The Sierra Club, an environmental organization active in the Bodega Bay antinuclear movement, described Bodega Bay as, "one of those places with a unique combination of sky, land, and water. It is a joy to the eye- a pleasure to behold!" (Bennett, 1963, p.4). As more information was released to the public, the primary argument of the Bodega Bay residents shifted to the proximity of the proposed site to the San Andreas Fault. The facility would be located less than a quarter of a mile away from the San Andreas Fault, the fault responsible for the devastating1906 earthquake in San Francisco (Walker, 1990, p. 329-330).

Even before the environmental impacts and health hazards of nuclear facilities were well known by the American public, there was apprehension regarding the presence of a nuclear power plant in a populated area. Between 1952 and 1964, there was one prominent study regarding nuclear power opinion in The United States published. The frequently cited statistics from this poll suggest that in 1956, 69% of residents surveyed were not concerned about a nuclear facility located within their community (Walker, 1990, p. 324). The procedure of this survey was not explicitly stated in the paper; it is likely that the methodology adhered to population survey criteria due to the vast number of individuals represented (LeCompte and Schensul, 2010). Two other nuclear power facilities in California faced similar opposition upon proposal, but both were fully constructed. The Diablo Canyon plant and the San Onofre plant are found on the California coastline, not unlike where the proposed Bodega Plant would have stood.

Nuclear power disasters such as Three Mile Island, Chernobyl, and Fukushima Daiichi have all reinforced the fears held by Bodega Bay residents. In fact, those opposing the PG&E facility in Bodega Bay noted that simply mentioning the year 1906, in reference to the catastrophic earthquake, was enough to inspire apprehension, if not fear, in Bodega Bay residents (Bennett, 1963, p. 4). As recognized by anthropologist Andrew Brooks, attention is brought to nuclear discourse when there is a disaster, but there is a need for an anthropological perspective in the field due to the incredibly social nature of nuclear power (2012, p. 137). The Bodega Bay antinuclear movement provides invaluable anthropological insight regarding how small communities are affected by the proposal of nuclear power facility construction. While the discourse in this case draws upon the threat of a nuclear disaster, it also draws attention to the impact the presence of a facility has on the population for purposes that are not related to nuclear health hazards.

Both the evolution of technology and the evolution of environmental consciousness contributed to the Bodega Bay antinuclear movement, as well as the campaigns against the Diablo Canyon and San Onofre facilities. The residents of these California coastal towns took advantage of changing perception of nuclear power to try to encourage their neighbors to support the prevention of nuclear power facility construction. Contemporary studies of the Diablo Canyon facility highlight population opinions and quantitative studies. One such study conducted in 1968 measures the opinion of San Luis Obispo County residents about the Diablo Canyon facility, and sorts the results by demographic (George and Southwell, 1986, p. 723-735). This survey was designed to obtain public opinion, gauge resident's opinion of proximity to the nuclear facility, and to determine if there are patterns among specific demographics in San Luis Obispo County (George and Southwell, 1986, p. 724). Previous studies showed that public awareness of nuclear power was primarily associated with support for the concept of nuclear power, so the researchers hoped to see if these beliefs were held within a community in which the nuclear facility was located (George and Southwell, 1986, p.724). Of 658 individuals eighteen and older, 64% responded to the survey, which focused on the whether or not Pacific Gas & Electric should have the right to continue operating the Diablo Canyon facility (George and Southwell, 1986, 725). The researchers then compared the data collected from the survey with the 1980 population census. This methodology is characteristic of a sample survey, in which data are gathered from a fraction of the population and are used to determine the general beliefs of the entire population (LeCompte and Schensul, 2010). The researchers used probit analysis to break down the demographics of the responses, citing variables such as health risks, income, age, sex, education, political ideology, and whether or not they had children (George and Southwell, 1986, 728).

The research conducted on the Bodega Bay antinuclear movement primarily involves the use of ethnographic interviews and content analysis. These techniques are the most appropriate methods of analysis of the Bodega Bay incident for a few reasons. Ethnographic interviews focus on a single informant, and due to the highly localized nature of this environmental conflict, the participants were never officially representative of a larger population (LeCompte and Schensul, 2010). In fact, the President of the California Public Utilities commission even acknowledged the lack of an official public opinion, and instead referred to the general impression given by Bodega Bay residents (Bennett, 1963, 3). Content analysis has proven to be useful because of the collection of letters, articles, and photographs from the movement, many have been preserved for future study (LeCompte and Schensul, 2010).

Some of the common ideologies, themes, and concepts found among the rhetoric used in nuclear power discourse universally include invoking associations with war, forcing labels on participants, and referencing nuclear power disasters. World War II influenced the perception of nuclear power. One particularly counterintuitive example found in literature of the era included a reference to the "glamour" of atomic energy, in wake of the World War II "atomic age" (P.H.A, 1962, p. 1231). War analogies became popular, and phrases like "The Battle of Bodega Bay" are in use to this day (Conzett, n.d.) In 1977, the LA Times published a picture of the San Onofre antinuclear protest. The subject of the photograph was a man holding a sign stating, "Nukes No, SolarCal Yes" (Meyer, 1977). This attitude has been prominent in antinuclear movements since then. After the Fukushima Daiichi disaster of 2011, citizens of Japan have taken to the streets to protest the nuclear industry. One news outlet noted one of the signs, which read, "No More Nukes" (Saito, 2014).

Another universally present element of nuclear rhetoric includes the labeling of opposing sides of the issue. The Sierra Club was an association whose participation was critical in the execution of the protest, but they were not exclusively devoted to the Bodega Bay cause. In 1957, prior to fighting PG&E in Bodega Bay, this environmental group noted that its members who identified as conservationists were at one point accused of perpetuating "neo-Malthusian" ideology (Wellock, 1992, p. 198). In response, executive director David Brower clarified that the stance of the Sierra Club was, "not blind opposition to progress, but of opposition to blind progress" (Wellock, 1992, p. 198). The manner in which antinuclear participants identified themselves or were labeled by others reflected the political atmosphere during the late 1950s and early 1960s. These associations were likely facilitated by the postwar environmental era mentioned previously in this analysis (Walker, 1990, p. 347). In fact, historian J. Samuel Walker notes that he suspects the Bodega Bay case may have proven to activists everywhere that environmental issues could be taken seriously (1990, p. 347). This seems to have been a turning point among environmentally conscious activists.

The threat of nuclear disaster is consistently found in most cases of antinuclear rhetoric. For example, one author associated with the San Onofre antinuclear movement published a satirical article describing a fictional scenario in which a terrorist infiltrated the San Onofre Nuclear Generating Station and sabotaged the facility, essentially turning it into a massive weapon (Schleimer, 1974, p. 24-27). Schleimer insists that public access to sensitive details about the plant placed those in close proximity of the facility in danger; the fictional death toll totaled 3,000 people, and stated that over 50,000 were exposed to radiation (1974, p.24).

The rhetoric of the Bodega Bay case has unique qualities because antinuclear movement was one of the first of its kind and because the incident was a localized phenomenon. Because the movement was a new incident, innovative campaign strategies were employed by the opposition. The antinuclear activists used creative methods to enrich their campaigns, including the use of song and bumper stickers. Jazz musician Lu Watters composed a song titled, "Blues over Bodega" to show his support for the antinuclear campaign, which received a lot of airtime on local radio stations (Walker, 1990, p. 336; Wellock, 1992, p. 205). He later appealed to supporters of PG&E's plans by contributing his opinion in the Santa Rosa Press Democrat in 1963, by explaining that constructing a nuclear facility so close to an area with known seismic activity made, "about as much sense as building an ammunition dump on the rim of Mount Vesuvius" (Conzett, n.d.). One of the more memorable forms of advertisement of the opposition was the use of bumper stickers, according to Bodega Bay resident Ned Mantua (Mantua, 2015).

Satirical approaches to this campaign quickly became far more involved and intricate than residents expected. Signs welcoming tourists to the *Bodega Bay Atomic Park* were posted on Bodega Head, drawing attention to the daunting prospect of altering the scenic view with industrial development (Wellock, 1992, p. 192). One tactic that has resonated with antinuclear activists throughout the years involved a demonstration of the widespread effects of nuclear fallout. At an outdoor meeting, participants released 1500 balloons at Bodega Head. Each of these balloons contained a message which read, "This balloon could represent a radioactive molecule of Strontium 90 or Iodine 131. PG&E hopes to build a nuclear plant at this spot, close to the world's biggest active earthquake fault. Tell your local newspaper where you found this balloon" (Walker, 1990, p. 336). At the time, this approach was unique and even considered controversial.

Another way that Bodega Bay proved to be a unique case could be seen by examining the transparency, or lack thereof, of PG&E's actions. In one instance, a proponent of nuclear power collaborated with authors who were responding to an article published that expressed contentment with the construction of the Bodega Bay facility. The new article featured the proponent retracting his support because he was not aware of the controversy (Peterson, Hedgpeth, Neilands, Pesonen, and P.H.A., 1963, p. 1121-1122; P.H.A., 1962). Another noted "procedural misdeed" was the blatant disregard of the 1,300 petitions submitted from residents (Wellock, 1992, p. 196). Pacific Gas and Electric began construction without permits while ignoring the rights of the community members. Yet another instance of "procedural misdeeds" was the severely inadequate analysis of Bodega Head as a suitable foundation for a nuclear plant (Wellock, 1992, p. 207). A popular quote used to diffuse Pacific Gas and Electric's credibility is attributed to Pierre Saint-Amand, a seismologist from the United States Geographic Survey expressed concern, explaining, "A worse foundation situation would be difficult to envision (Walker, 1990, p. 337)". Walker notes that this quote was highlighted as front-page news in San Francisco Bay Area newspapers, radio stations, and television programs (1990, p. 337). Nuclear power opponents would focus their campaigns on the legislative misdeeds of Pacific Gas and Electric, using this quote and phrases criticizing the science behind their location choice.

The most prominent and enduring term to result from the Bodega Bay antinuclear movement is the "Hole in the Head", a reference to the pit in Bodega Head and the needlessness of nuclear power fifty miles north of San Francisco. This phrase originated in 1964, not long after PG&E was forced to abandon plans for construction of the nuclear facility; activist David Pesonen initiated

"Empty Hole in the Head" day in celebration (Wellock, 1992, p. 208). The Hole in the Head is still there to this day, although it is now a pond.

I have found that nuclear power activism rhetoric has changed over time, and that strategies used in the Bodega Bay movement can be found in contemporary antinuclear movements. The most prominent manner in which nuclear rhetoric has changed over time can best be demonstrated by comparing the first and last examples discussed in this paper chronologically. While the Bodega Bay nuclear activists had to fight for recognition of the dangers of nuclear facilities in close proximity to fault lines, Japanese residents after the Fukushima Daiichi disaster of 2011 did not need to speculate how severely the effects of seismic activity would destabilize nuclear reactors. One protester at a rally encouraging the end of the nuclear industry described how radiation affected her daily life. It drastically altered if she could eat, if she could leave her house, if she and her children could safely move about without air mask: she had even referred to herself as a *hibakusha*, which is a term used to describe a survivor of the atomic bombs dropped in Japan during World War II (Ogawa, 2013, p. 319). Similarly, many people residing in Satsumasendai, a Japanese town with a nearby nuclear facility, adopted a less favorable opinion of the nuclear power industry after the devastating Fukushima incident (Saito, 2014). However, they implemented a familiar tactic to raise awareness for their cause: they released balloons exactly as the Bodega Bay residents did nearly fifty years earlier in order to indicate how far radioactive molecules could travel if there were a nuclear disaster (Saito, 2014). The genre of satire, like in the Bodega Bay case, has been a useful tool in more contemporary antinuclear protests.

It has been more than fifty-five years since the Bodega Bay protesters illuminated the dangers of nuclear power facilities, especially those constructed in locations with known seismic activity.

The Fukushima disaster reinforced this notion. Bodega Bay set a precedent for a successful antinuclear campaign structure. Future studies on the topic should compare and contrast antinuclear movements, not just nuclear facility disasters. While these disasters are crucial to antinuclear discourse and provide substantial support for claims of health and safety hazards that accompany nuclear facilities, it is apparent that discerning themes from the campaigns themselves has not been a prominent aspect of study. Finding parallels within different campaign rhetorical structure reveals a lot about the communities in question, and could potentially aid in supporting or preventing the construction of nuclear facilities.

The Bodega Bay ordeal was not entirely without harm. Today, the Hole in the Head serves as a reminder that the innovation and perseverance of the dedicated antinuclear movement participants protected not only their scenic view of the Pacific Ocean, but possibly the lives of generations to come.

REFERENCES

Bennett, W. (1963, July 26). The Dissenting Opinion. *Bodega Bay Atomic Park*, 1-11.

Brooks, A. (2012). Radiating Knowledge: The Public Anthropology of Nuclear Energy. *American Anthropologist, 114*(1), 137-140.

Conzett, N. (n.d.). The Battle of Bodega Bay.

LeCompte, M., & Schensul, J. (2010). *Designing and Conducting Ethnographic Research: An Introduction (Ethnographer's Toolkit, Second Edition)*. AltaMira Press.

Mantua, N. (2015, March 22). [Personal interview].

Meyer, R. (1977, August 7). Image, *LA Times*.

Ogawa, A. (2013). Young precariat at the forefront: Anti-nuclear rallies in post-Fukushima Japan. Inter-Asia Cultural Studies, 14(2), 317-326.

Peterson, M., Hedgpeth, J., Neilands, J., Pesonen, D., & P.H.A. (1963). Bodega Bay Nuclear Plant. *Science, 139*(3559), 1117-1122.

P.H.A. (1962). Civilian Nuclear Power. *Science, 138*(3546), 1231-1231.

Saito, M. (2014, April 3). In post-Fukushima policy test, Japan town rallies for nuclear re-start.

Schleimer, J. (1974). The day they blew up San Onofre. *Bulletin of the Atomic Scientists, 30*(8), 24-27.

Walker, J. (1990). Reactor at the Fault: The Bodega Bay Nuclear Plant Controversy, 1958-1964: A Case Study in the Politics of Technology. *Pacific Historical Review, 59*(3), 323-348.

Wellock, T. (1992). The Battle for Bodega Bay: The Sierra Club and Nuclear Power, 1958-1964. *California History, 71*(2), 192-211.

CAPTIVE MANDRILLS' (*MANDRILLUS SPHINX*)

CORE BEHAVIORAL NEEDS AT THE SAN FRANCISCO ZOO:

A NEED FOR BEHAVIORAL ENRICHMENT

KYLE RUNZEL

ANTHROPOLOGY MAJOR

SONOMA STATE UNIVERSITY

ABSTRACT

Zoos have a responsibility to meet animals' physical needs by providing appropriate temperature, space, and nutrition. Zoos must bear in mind that they are the "giants" whose "shadows" can inspire exploration and growth in their non-human tenants. According to Watters (unpublished manuscript), zoos also have a responsibility to meet animals' core behavioral needs. Animals whose physical and behavioral needs are met are more likely to have reduced fear and anxiety, be more responsive to training, and display a greater diversity of behaviors. I observed a group of mandrills (N=4) housed at the San Francisco Zoo for 20 hours between March 1 and April 22, 2014 to assess their ability to express their core behavioral needs: investigating, acquiring reward, and exerting control. I recorded the focal animal's behavior and location using instantaneous sampling with 1-minute intervals. The mandrills display variation in the behaviors expressed, but the most common behaviors were feeding and foraging, resting, auto-grooming and walking. One female, Lulu, spent 13.5% of her interval samples engaged in hair-plucking, indicating that her core behavioral needs are currently unmet. These baseline data suggest that the San Francisco Zoo mandrills will benefit from behavioral enrichment.

Key Words: Behavior, Captive, Enrichment, Hair-plucking, Mandrill, San Francisco Zoo, Stereotype

INTRODUCTION

How is social behavior (or lack thereof) and enclosure use contributing to Lulu's (a mandrill at the San Francisco Zoo) self-directed plucking? Using Jason Watter's definition of core behavioral needs as a basis for categorizing positive and negative behaviors, a graphical representation can be made to understand Lulu's stereotypy behavior in relation to her enrichment at the San Francisco Zoo. Three female mandrills and one male mandrill at the San Francisco Zoo were observed for a total of 20 hours. The observations were done between March 1st, 2014 and April 22nd, 2014. Data collected using the instantaneous focal sampling method with 1 minute time intervals. Each observation period was 20 minutes and done on both weekdays and weekends. With each minute, the location and behavior performed would be recorded. The most common behaviors recorded include feeding and foraging, resting, auto-grooming, and walking off. Although plucking only consisted of 3.14% of the total intervals, Lulu spent 13.5% of her intervals plucking. Lulu also spent over half of her intervals in a single quadrat. Lulu has a higher percent of intervals in quadrat 3 than any of the other subjects. Using Watters description of core behavioral needs Lulu's behaviors would classify as negative in both investigating and exerting control, but positive in the category acquiring reward. With the collective data, I believe Lulu's negative experiences in exerting control is related to her negative investigative behavior and enclosure use. She lacks an enriching experience from her enclosure and, therefore, is not in a healthy state of psychological well-being

Primates are highly social creatures with relatively large brains compared to body size (Dunbar, 1992). Like humans, primates need to exercise and enrich both their brains and their bodies to maintain a healthy lifestyle. Considerable amounts of research have been spent on both behavioral and environmental enrichment for primates in order to keep their psychological well-being healthy

(Chang et al., 1999). This type of research is important because it can both benefit and maintain the overall health and mental well-being of primates living in captivity (Hosey, 2004) and zoo "enclosures are still in need of improvement" to stimulate captive animals (Fabregas et al., 2012). Mandrills (*Mandrillus sphinx*) are highly social primates which fall into the taxonomic order of Catarrhini, otherwise known as Old World monkeys and the subfamily Cercopithicinae. Mandrills especially need environmental and social stimulation since they live within "a complex multimale-multifemale social organization" (Charpentier et al., 2005) in the wild. These social groups can range from 15 individuals up to a horde of 845 individuals in the jungles in Cameroon and neighboring countries (Abernethy, 2002). It is extremely difficult to replicate the population size and habitat in captive settings, making captive mandrills live in very different settings than they are biologically meant to be. Captive primates also encounter the mental stress which comes from excessive amounts of stimulation from visitors (Chamove et al., 1988). Although there are considerable amounts of research on mandrills, there is still little known about their natural and captive social and psychological well-being.

It is common for stereotypes such as hair plucking, otherwise known as hair pulling, to appear from "animals who are confined in an artificial environment" (Reinhardt, 2005) such as enclosures at a zoo. Hair plucking is defined in this study, as seen in table 1, as the pulling out of hairs on any part of the body.

Table 1

Ethogram		
Code	*Term*	*Definition*
app	Approach	Moves within 2-3 ft. of another individual
	Search	Manipulates environment in look for specific object
supp	Supplant	Approachee leaves area and approacher takes place
	Chase	Running rapidly after another individual
	Fight	Hits, grabs, jumps on, or bites another individual
	Stare	Directed gaze at another mandrill (held for 3 sec)
avd	Avoid	Moves away from approacher in a walk or run
hd shk	Head Shake	Head movement when presented by another
pres	Present	Purposely turning posterior to an individual submissively
	Mount	Male approaches female and climbs on top of her
copul	Copulate	Male mounts female, inserts penis and thrusts with pause for ejaculation
un copul	Unsuccessful Copulate	Male mounts female, inserts penis and thrusts and ends without a pause for ejaculation
	Groom	Lick hair pick skin of another individual
f&f	Feeding & Foraging	Finding and consuming food
	Rest	Any period of inactivity, seated or standing, eyes open or closed
mast	Masturbate	Male sexually stimulates himself
autogr	Autogroom	Licks hair or picks skin of self
	Pluck	Pulling out hairs of any body part

Such stereotypic behavior is an indicator of stress in the psychological well-being of animals, especially in non-human primates. Hair pulling has been identified in multiple species of primates in captivity, which includes baboons, chimpanzees, rhesus macaques, squirrel monkeys, (Reinhardt, 2005) and mandrills. In captivity "there is considerable evidence that primates housed under impoverished conditions develop behavioral abnormalities, including, in the most extreme example, self-harming behavior" such as hair plucking (Honess et al., 2006).

Table 2

Core Behavioral Needs	Experiences	
	Positive	Negative
Investigating	Feed & Forage	Rest
	Search	Auto-groom
Acquiring Reward	Copulate	Unsuccessful Copulate
	Groom	
	Masturbate	
Exerting Control	Approach	Pluck Hair
	Avoid	
	Supplant	
	Chase	
	Stare	
	Headshake	
	Present	
	Mount	
	Fight	

This study asks, are the mandrills at the San Francisco Zoo being environmentally stimulated by their enclosure and is their psychological well-being in a healthy state? First, observations of the mandrill's spatial use in their enclosure were used to determine if they are being environmentally stimulated. The measure of space use is important to determine how appropriate a captive environment is for the subject (Ross et al., 2009). Next, the types of behaviors that appeared were noted and the frequency of social and nonsocial behaviors the mandrills had was analyzed. This was used to determine the amount of social interactions the mandrills are displaying.

Using Jason Watters definition of core behavioral needs, the behaviors were categorized as positive or negative behaviors in the categories; investigate, acquiring reward, and exerting control to determine the mandrill's well-being as seen in table 2. Meeting a captive animals' core behavioral needs allows animals to maintain their mental well-being, reduce fear, be more responsive to training, and creating a better guest experience by engaging with their captive environment (Watters, ND). According to Jason Watters, captive animals have a need to seek opportunities and information, reach desired outcomes, and manage the process in which they reach those outcomes (Watters, ND). Although positive experiences are supported, it is unrealistic to believe negative experiences would not occur. It is important for captive animals to keep a balance between positive and negative experiences. While excessive negative behaviors indicates a need for improvement in an animals mental welfare, an excessive amount of positive behaviors will anticipate events and lead to boredom and support stereotypy behaviors such as pacing. Finally, this study looks for possible techniques to stimulate and enrich the mandrills through improving their enclosure use.

MATERIALS AND METHODS

SUBJECTS AND SITE

The individuals observed were 3 female mandrills and 1 male mandrill at the San Francisco Zoo, San Francisco, California. The 3 females are named Angie (21-22 years old), Dora (21-22 years old), and Lulu (10 years old). The male in the enclosure is named Jesse (15-16 years old). Angie, Dora, and Lulu were all originally part of a social group in an enclosure at the San Diego Zoo. It should be noted that Lulu was brought to the zoo first, at a very young age with her mother and another male. After the death of Lulu's mother and the transfer of the other male, Jesse was introduced. Angie and Dora were then brought from the San Diego Zoo in an attempt to reconnect with Lulu and proceed to socialize with her. The subjects are in a circular pit-style enclosure filled with various vegetation and boulders.

PROCEDURE

Exactly 20 hours of observation were conducted at the mandrill enclosure at the San Francisco Zoo & Gardens. The observations were done between March 1st, 2014 and April 22nd, 2014 between the hours of 10:00 A.M. and 4:00 P.M. Each observation period was 20 minutes and done on both weekdays and weekends. Before starting observations, the observer took an hour to familiarize himself with the subjects and the types of behaviors he would be expecting to see. Next, the enclosure was sketched in order to draw out where to place the predetermined quadrats proportionally as shown in figure 1.

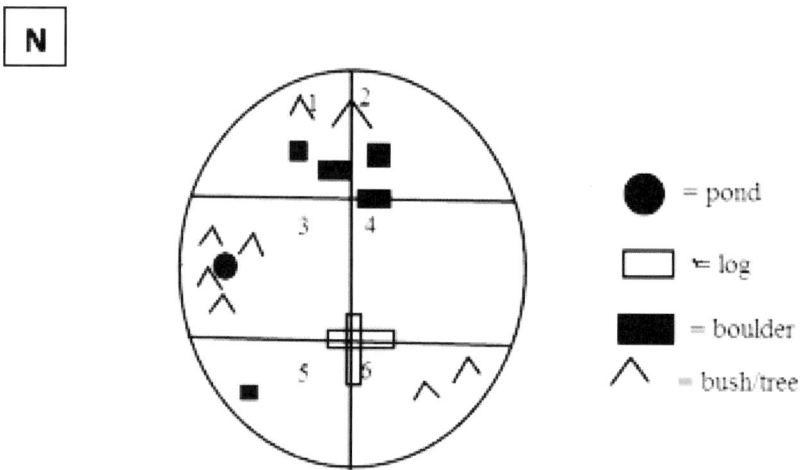

Figure 1

The enclosure was divided into six similarly sized quadrats to determine the spatial location of the mandrills in the enclosure. Next, using a stopwatch and a database template, titled HanDbase, which is uploaded into a smart-phone, the data was collected using the instantaneous focal sampling method with 1 minute time intervals. With each minute, both the quadrat the subject occupied and the behavior performed were recorded. After collecting 2-4 hours of data each day, the data would be directly uploaded into an Excel spread sheet and eliminating possible bias in transcribing data incorrectly from printed data collecting sheets to an Excel spread sheet for analysis.

ANALYSIS

Each visit to the enclosure would yield approximately 2 to 4 hours of recorded observations. Each of the 4 subjects were observed a total of 15 times, equaling a total of 60 observations made. Each individual was observed for 20 minutes at a time and observed each focal 15 times, which makes a total of 300 minutes (5 hours) of observation per an individual. Each focal was observed for exactly a quarter of the total 20 hours.

RESULTS

The most frequent recorded behavior was feeding and or foraging which consisted of 40.97% of all the mandrills total recorded behavioral intervals. The other most common behaviors recorded include resting (24.13%), auto grooming (9.52%), and search (11.71%). Although plucking only consisted of 3.14% of the total intervals, Lulu spent 13.5% of her intervals plucking. When looking at the frequency of social versus nonsocial behaviors, Angie has 244 of her recorded behavioral intervals categorized as nonsocial while Jesse and Dora both have 241 of their recorded behavioral intervals as nonsocial. Lulu has the highest frequency of a nonsocial behavior (257) as seen in figure 2. After categorizing the behaviors into Jason Watters' core behavioral needs, the recorded behavioral intervals show the mandrills have 14 positive and 1 negative experience in the acquiring reward category, 253 positive and 43 negative experiences in the exerting control category, and 519 positive and 424 negative behaviors in the investigation category as seen in figure 3. Lulu specifically had 58 positive and 43 negative behaviors in the exerting control category making her the sole contributor to the negative behaviors in the exerting control category for the mandrill groups core behavioral needs in frequency.

Mandrill Group's Behavior

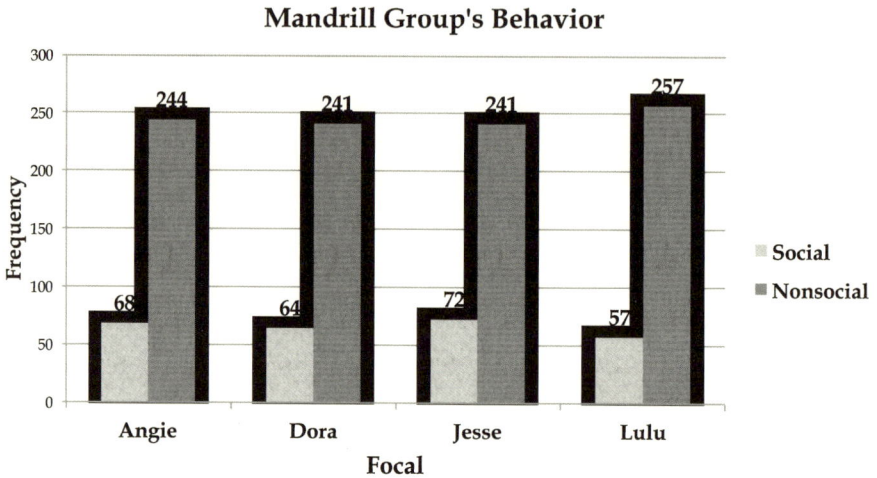

Figure 2

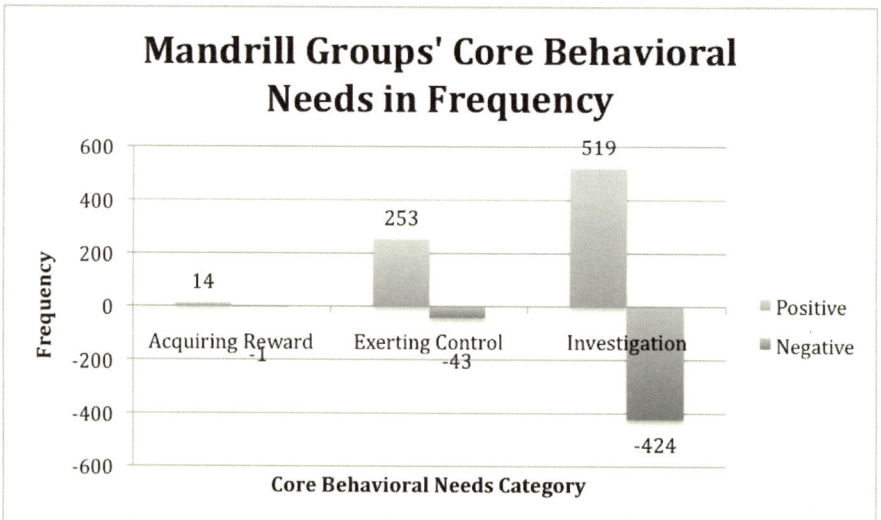

Figure 3

When reviewing the total quadrat usage intervals, the subjects had a large portion of their intervals in the western side of the enclosure, which consists of quadrats 1, 3, and 5 as labeled in figure 1. The subjects have 10% of their intervals in quadrat 1, 44.21% in quadrat 3 and 27.38% in quadrat 5. This makes a total of 81.59% of their recorded intervals in the western quadrats of the enclosure. Focusing again on Lulu, 65.40% of her recorded intervals placed her in quadrat 3 (fig. 4), meaning Lulu spent over half of her intervals in a specific quadrat. Lulu has a higher percent of intervals in quadrat 3 than any of the other subjects.

DISCUSSION

Examining the data collected, it is clear that the mandrills have a high preference for the western quadrats of the enclosure. Referring back to figure 1, the preference to the western enclosure may be influenced by the amount of cover from bushes as well as being the only area containing the only known water source in the enclosure. The bush cover provides them with the ability to hide from the zoo visitors, as well as the other mandrills in the enclosure. This may link to why Lulu performs antisocial and stereotypical behavior such as hair plucking while spending the majority of her intervals in quadrat 3. Both the quadrat uses and core behavioral needs frequencies show the mandrills, especially Lulu, are not investigating and exploring their captive environment. This excessive amount of negative experiences in her investigative core behavioral need suggests her mental well-being is not healthy. Since she is not moving from quadrats often and is not displaying a healthy amount of investigative behaviors, Lulu has little opportunities to interact with the other mandrills especially since they are not moving and investigating as often as they should. This lack of social behavior may be providing enough opportunity to exert her stereotypy behavior of plucking. The use of environmental enrichment may increase the amount of investigation and social behavior between her and the other mandrills enough to distract her from plucking her hair. Enrichment may not eliminate the behavior directly but it can distract Lulu enough to focus on other behavioral need of investigating and improve her mental well-being enough to give her the mental capability to exert control over her hair plucking. In zoos, there are many technological applications that are being used to increase both the visitors experience and the well-being of the primates (Clay et al., 2011). One possible recommendation I would suggest for future projects is to include using a feeder to have the mandrills feed and forage in lesser used quadrats. I also recommend trying to make the enclosure as natural as possible since approximately 80% of enclosures were dubbed unsuitable by Fabregas, et al. (2012) due to a lack of environmental similarities.

CONCLUSION

In conclusion, I believe the mandrills are bored and not stimulated by their enclosure. Looking at the most common types of behaviors they perform, it is clear they spend most of their intervals not being socially active. Lulu being the most extreme case with 65.40% of her intervals taking place in only 1 quadrat, the majority of her behavior is not only non-social, and stereotypical, but she is socially isolated from the other mandrills most of the time. Bettinger (1994) concludes that other social primates, such as chimpanzees, having areas to isolate themselves is beneficial to their well-being since they can hide from visitors. However, I find that is not the case with highly social creatures like the mandrills at the San Francisco Zoo. Mandrills have been known to live in large hordes of up to 845 (Abernethy, 2002) and face large amounts of social stimulation in the wild yet the mandrills at the San Francisco Zoo spend 79% of their total recorded behavioral intervals performing nonsocial behaviors. Like Chamove (1988), I believe "there is clearly no simple way of predicting which species of primate is most likely to be influenced by the presence of an audience". Little stimulation from both the enclosure and the other mandrills impact Lulu's psychological well-being, resulting in her focusing more on performing stereotypical behavior such as hair plucking which is harmful to her physical well-being. According to Jason Watters' core behavioral needs, the mandrills are all displaying an excessive amount of negative behaviors in the investigation category which suggests they are not exploring, moving, and therefore not making social contact as often as they should to maintain a healthy mental well-being. Lulu especially needs these social distractions since nearly half of her behavior in the exerting control category is plucking. The application of "methods to reduce or eliminate stereotypes from occurring in zoo animals are of primary importance" since it can help the over-all health of a primate (Shyne, 2006). With the collective data, I believe the mandrills at the San Francisco Zoo lack an enriching experience from their enclosure and, therefore, are not in a healthy state of psychological well-being. Additional factors, which may contribute to their psychological well-being, could be ruled out with further study.

REFERENCES

Abernethy, K. A., White, L. J. T., & Wickings, E. J. (2002). Hordes of mandrills (*mandrillus sphinx*): extreme group size and seasonal male presence. *Journal of Zoology*, 258, 131-137.

Bettinger, T., Wallis, J., Carter, T. (1994). Spatial selection in captive adult female chimpanzees. Zoo Biology, 13, 67-176.

Chamove, A.S., Hosey, G. R., Schaetzel, P. (1988). Visitors excite primates in zoos. Zoo Biology, 7, 359-369.

Chang, T. R., Forthman, D. L., Maple, T. L. (1999). Comparison of confined mandrills (Mandrillus sphinx) behavior in traditional and "ecologically representative" exhibits. Zoo Biology, 18, 163-176.

Charpentier, M., Peignot, P., Gimenez, O., et al. (2005). Constraints on control: factors influencing reproductive success in male mandrills (Mandrillus sphinx). Behavioral Ecology, 16, 614-623.

Clay, A. W., Perdue, B. M., Gaalema, D. E., et al. (2011). The use of technology to enhance zoological parks. Zoo Biology, 30, 487-497.

Dunbar, R. I. M. (1992). Neocortex size as a constraint on group size in primates. Journal of Human Evolution, 20, 469-493.

Fabregas, M. C., Guillen-Salazar, F., Garces-Naro, C. (2012). Do naturalistic enclosures provide suitable environments for zoo animals?. Zoo Biology, 31, 362-373.

Honess, P. E., Marin, C. M. (2006). Enrichment and aggression in primates. Neuroscience and Biobehavioral Reviews, 30, 413-436.

Hosey, G.R. (2004). How does the zoo environment affect the behavior of captive primates? Applied Animal Behaviour Science, 90, 107-129.

Reinhardt, V. (2005). Hair pulling: a review. Laboratory Animals, 39, 361-369.

Ross, S.R., Schapiro, S.J., Hua, J., Lukas, K. E. (2009). Space use as an indicator of enclosure appropriateness: a novel measure of captive animal welfare. Applied Animal Behaviour Science, 121, 42-50.

Shyne, A. (2006). Meta-analytical review of the effects of enrichment on stereotypic behavior in zoo mammals. Zoo Biology, 25, 317-337.

Watters, J. (ND). Animals' core behavioral needs. Unpublished Manuscript.

ENCLOSURE USE IN A CAPTIVE ALL-MALE GROUP
OF SQUIRREL MONKEYS (SAIMIRI SCIUREUS)

MADELINE WARNEMENT

ENVIRONMENTAL STUDIES AND PLANNING MAJOR

SONOMA STATE UNIVERSITY

ABSTRACT

In the wild, common squirrel monkeys, *Saimiri sciureus,* are found in multi-male/multi-female groups (Boinski 1999) and aggression between males is common, often resulting in disfiguring scars (Boinski et al. 2002). In biomedical research, squirrel monkeys are listed as the second most frequently utilized research subject (Jack 2011), yet many are euthanized after their research utility ends because zoos are reluctant to house all-male groups for fear of serious injuries and death (C. MacDonald, pers. comm.). The purpose of this project is to study the behavior and enclosure use of one of the largest all-male groups of squirrel monkeys housed at an AZA-accredited facility. I collected 50 hours of behavioral data using five-minute focal samples with 30-second intervals. Every 30 seconds, I recorded the focal animal's behavior and location in the enclosure. I will describe how individual squirrel monkeys use the enclosure and how this use has changed over time. My results indicate that there is variation in enclosure use among individual monkeys. These results may be used by the San Francisco Zoo, and perhaps other zoos, to more effectively manage all-male groups of squirrel monkeys in the future.

Key Words: Animal behavior, Enclosure use,
Saimiri sciureus, Squirrel Monkeys,

BACKGROUND

In the wild squirrel monkeys live in heterosexual groups ranging from 15 to 30 individuals (Boinski 1999). Males from the group will often fight to prevent other males from joining the group (Boinski 2005). These fights can often result in disfiguring scars.

In captivity squirrel monkeys are the second most utilized biomedical research subject (Jack 2011). The females along with some males are kept for breeding purposes leaving a surplus of males. It is often thought that male squirrel monkeys will be more aggressive in captivity than in the wild because of limited space. These males are therefore often euthanized because of difficulty finding a place for them to retire.

My research took place at the San Francisco Zoo, where there is currently a group of 15 squirrel monkeys that were previously used as a biomedical research group. At the previous facility they were kept in groups of two so they did not know each other until they arrived at the San Francisco Zoo. The primate keepers were apprehensive to see what would happen when all of the monkeys would be introduced in one enclosure instead of sharing space with only one other individual. The zoo enclosure has both an inside portion and outside portion of the enclosure. The monkeys are allowed access to all of the enclosure 24 hours a day (i.e. they are never confined to one part of the enclosure at any one point in time).

RESEARCH QUESTION

With the assumption that male squirrel monkeys would be inherently aggressive in captivity as they are in the wild, the primate keepers as well as other zoo staff were nervous about what would happen when they took on this group of, originally, 20 squirrel monkeys. This brought up the question; can an all-male group of squirrel monkeys be successfully housed in captivity?

METHODS OF COLLECTION

Data was collected on an iPad using an application called HanDBase. This application can be tailored to the specific needs of the person and may be set up in any fashion. Once the data has been collected, it can be uploaded right to Excel. It eliminates the need to collect data by hand on sheets of paper and enter in data to Excel manually. Below is a picture of the home screen of the application (on the left) and a map of the enclosure (on the right). Inside the white column on the home page is the list of behaviors and next to that is the location button that would then take me to the map of the enclosure. One individual would be observed every five minutes. Every 30 seconds within those five minutes, behavior and location were recorded as well as weather. The data in this paper is from August 2013 to November 2014 and shows 54.24 hours of data.

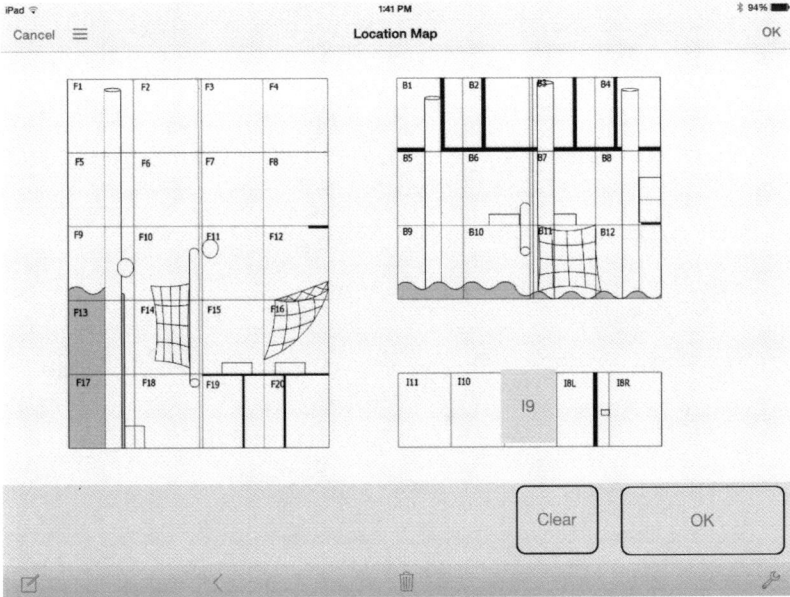

QUADRAT USE

When analyzing quadrat use, to make it easier to understand, the quadrats were grouped together by rows. The enclosure is split up into the front, back, and inside. There were two sets of quadrats that were utilized more than any other: F13-F16 where they spent 35% of their time, and B5-B8 where they spent 26% of their time. Below is a graph that displays the percent of time all quadrats were used.

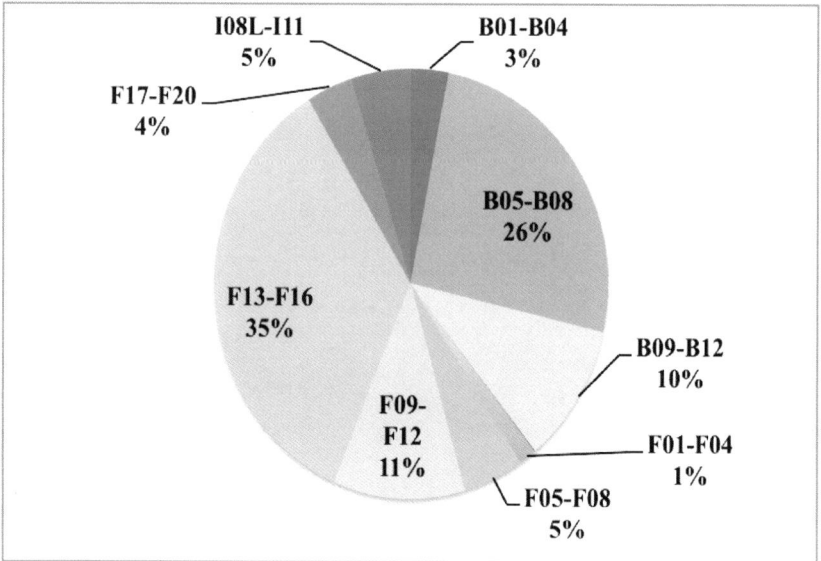

BREAKDOWN OF BEHAVIOR

Once it was determined where the monkeys were spending most of their time, next another question came up; what behaviors are being exhibiting in these quadrats? As displayed by the graphs below there are three dominant behaviors being observed. Rest, feed/forage, and locomote arboreal in both F13-F16 and B5-B8 are dominant. Rest is 44% for the front quadrats and 46% for the back quadrats. Feed/forage is 39% for the front quadrats and 20% for the back quadrats. Locomote arboreal is 11% for the front quadrats and 18% for the back quadrats. What is special about F13-F16 and B5-B8 is that these are the only quadrats in the enclosure that have heating pads, heating lamps, and food in all of these quadrats. It follows that they are spending so much time resting and feed/foraging in these areas. If they are not resting or feed/foraging they are locomoting. Note that in the graphs shown below, any behavior that was exhibited 0% of the time was not included in the image.

F13-F16 Behaviors

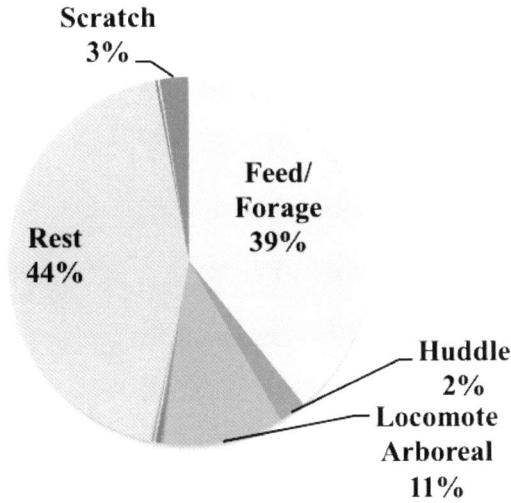

Scratch
3%

Feed/
Forage
39%

Rest
44%

Huddle
2%

Locomote
Arboreal
11%

B5-B8 Behaviors

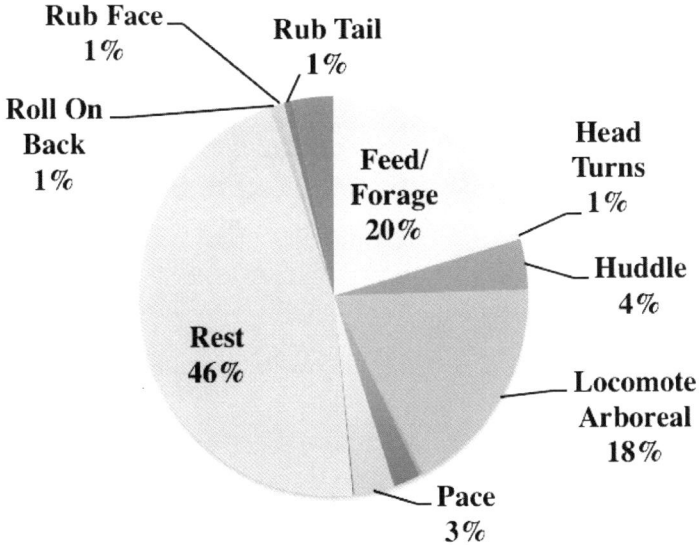

Rub Face
1%

Rub Tail
1%

Roll On
Back
1%

Head
Turns
1%

Feed/
Forage
20%

Huddle
4%

Rest
46%

Locomote
Arboreal
18%

Pace
3%

In comparison with the overall behavior, the behaviors displayed in F13-F16 and B5-B8 were very similar to the behaviors overall. In the overall behavior, rest was 41.5%, feed/forage was 31.0%, and locomote arboreal was 18%. On closer look at the overall behavior, the behavior of concern in this research, aggression, took up only 0.7% of their time. Within that 0.7% only 16% of the aggression was high intensity, meaning physical aggression. The other 84% was low intensity aggression, meaning any other negative behavior associated with aggression or dominance. The majority of their physical contact was in huddling, which these monkeys do for warmth. They huddle due to the cold weather in San Francisco and are usually only seen huddling on cold days. These monkeys in particular are not very social. They keep to themselves and each individual has a space in the enclosure that they gravitate towards. There is no grooming or playing as it might be suspected. There is often little to no physical contact.

When the zoo first got the monkeys, aggression was higher, as expected with any animal. This initial aggression in animals is often a result of the struggle to establish a dominance hierarchy. In this particular group of animals, it was seen that over time aggression went down and as of October 2013 there were no major injuries. The total amount of injuries overall is going down as well to where we see almost no injuries occurring. According to the results and the graph shown below, there was more than once instance of no injuries recorded during that month. The rate of injuries is leveling off. Even in the beginning when the individuals were establishing dominance, the rate of major injuries was very low.

Documented Wounds

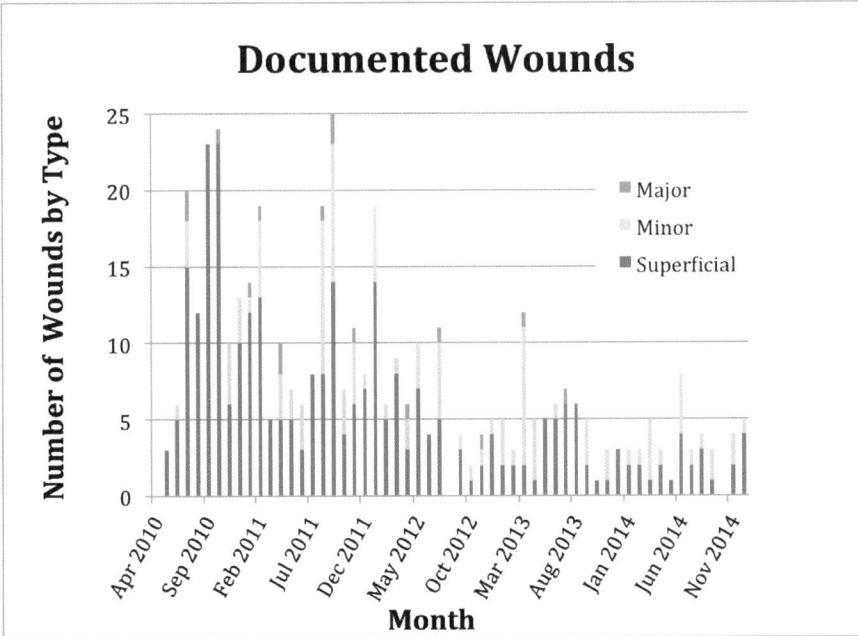

INSIDE USE

The main primate keeper, David Carol, noticed that many of the squirrel monkeys were not using the inside enclosure. David took data solely on the inside of the enclosure from August 2013 to January 2014. From this data it was concluded that the majority of the monkeys using the inside space were the more dominant monkeys. There are only two small doors that lead to the inside. On speaking with the keeper, David Carol, he observed that some of the dominant monkeys were keeping the less dominant monkeys from coming inside by sitting close to the doors leading inside. This deterred the less dominant monkeys from entering through these doors and therefore kept them outside. However, later on during this study David reported that he observed a good flow of different monkeys using the inside space, including some of the less dominant individuals. Monkeys that he had never seen inside, were observed coming and going more frequently. This is good progress for a group of this size. It means that they are maturing as a group and are becoming less confrontational. Now that they are all coming inside it also makes it easier to handle the group if they needed to all be inside for a safety or health reason. It is very useful for the keeper to be able to move the group wherever he may need them at any point in time.

CONCLUSIOns

After analyzing all of this data, it is clear that a group of all male squirrel monkeys can be housed successfully in captivity despite the aggression exhibited in the wild. Even though they show aggression often in the wild, they have not shown consistent aggression in captivity at the San Francisco Zoo. In the wild, heterosexual groups of squirrel monkeys there are many different outlying males challenging the males inside the group. The monkeys in captivity have time to get used to one another. There are no males from the outside trying to enter the group. The group dynamic in captivity is always constant, which can lower aggression over time once dominance has been established. In this group of captive squirrel monkeys, all of the individuals were males. Some of the reason for aggression in the wild is to protect the females and keep the outlying male monkeys from mating with their females. However, in this particular captive group there were no females to fight over. This could also be a factor of lower aggression in captivity. All of this, as well as the consistent work of the keeper to train the group and work with the group has all contributed to lower aggression. It is also important that there be multiple sources of food as well as sources of heat located in different areas of the cage. Since rest and feed/forage are such dominant behaviors, having different sources of food and heat go a long way in decreasing aggression because then there is no fight over which individual gets food or warmth.

As long as the group of squirrel monkeys is worked with on a regular basis, tracked for aggression, and given different places to feed/forage and rest, aggression over time should be kept to a minimum.

The hope is that these finding can help save squirrel monkeys from euthanasia and therefore find more places willing to retire these monkeys after use in biomedical research. The next steps would be to complete more analysis and to get the word out to other facilities that might have the opportunity to take on an all-male group of squirrel monkeys.

ACKNOWLEDGMENTS

Thanks to the people and grants that supported the SSUPER Lab and the squirrel monkey project without which none of this would have been possible, including, Provost's Undergraduate Research Grants, School of Social Sciences Summer Research Grant, International Primatological Society Captive Care Grant, and Marcia K. Brown Memorial Primatology Scholarship Fund. I would also like to thank my peers that participated in the SSUPER Lab. They were a good support system and I had a lot to learn from each one of them.

Thank you to the head of the Anthropology Department at Sonoma State University, Dr. Karin Jaffe. Without her enthusiasm and passion for primatology, and this project in particular, none of this would have been possible. She was a wonderful mentor as this research was conducted.

A big thanks to the San Francisco Zoo for allowing the opportunity to observe their squirrel monkeys as well as use their facilities and other resources. Thank you to David Carol, the primate keeper at the San Francisco Zoo, for spending so much time with me while I was trying to learn all the individuals and the quadrats of the enclosure. His enthusiasm for these animals, and his knowledge was inspiring.

Thank you to my parents as they supported me through my research of the squirrel monkeys. Thank you for sending me to Sonoma State University, for helping me through this research, and for being there for all the conferences I spoke at regarding this project.

Thank you lastly to Sonoma State for providing the resources and opportunity to participate in a program such as this.

REFERENCES

Boinski S. 1999. The social organization of squirrel monkeys: implications for ecological models of social evolution. Evolutionary Anthropology 8(3): 101-12.

Boinski S, Kauffman L, Ehmke E, Schet S, Vreedzaam A. 2005. Dispersal patterns among three species of squirrel monkeys (Saimiri oerstedii, S. boliviensis, and S. sciureus): Divergent costs and benefits. Behaviour 142(5): 525-632.

Jack KM. (2011). The Cebines: toward an explanation of variable social structure. In: Campbell CJ, Fuentes A, MacKinnon KC, Bearder SK, Stumpf RM, editors. Primates in perspective. Oxford University Press: New York. pp 108-122.

FOREWORD

TECHNOLOGY HIGH SCHOOL
PARTICIPANTS & RESEARCH

This year marks the first year of the *Society & Culture Undergraduate Research Forum* invited participants from Technology High School to participate, presenting their research in both in our forum and the journal publication. Technology High School is housed on the Sonoma State Campus, and focuses its instruction to prepare its students for the rigorous fields of math, science, and engineering. As the students are taught in smaller groups and more intensively, we felt they would eagerly want to participate in SCURF to prove themselves alongside undergraduate researchers.

Our forum event on April 15, 2015 showcased three separate poster presentations by Technology High School students within the larger 1st Annual Research Symposium. Marcos Carballal, Molly Melville, and Jose Moncada with Kobe Weinstein, all enthusiastically discussed their projects with the visitors and other presenters. We also featured an oral presentation by Zachary Miller, who impressed all of those present with his description of his independent research on natural growing methods in plants. All of these young researchers were nothing short of professional during the event.

In this journal, we proudly present the complete research of three of our Technology High participants and hope this experience encourages them to continue on in their academic journey. As their mentors, Horacio and I personally worked with each of these participants and are very proud of all of what they have achieved thus far. We encourage you to join us in the experience of what is to come for the future of undergraduate researchers.

Horacio Arcila & Lauren Russ
SCURF Advisors for Technology High School Participants

ANALYZING ORIGINS AND EFFECTS OF GENDER STEREOTYPES WITHIN TESTING ENVIRONMENTS

MARCOS CARBALLAL

SOPHOMORE

TECHNOLOGY HIGH SCHOOL

ABSTRACT

Throughout history, civilization has felt the need to classify its citizens. Although a seemingly natural urge, it does not appear beneficial to the advancement of society. Groups were established by demographic, and naturally, ideas developed about each group. However, people would assign qualities to an entire group that only applies to part of a group. Also, members subject to these stereotypes are often dissociative to their own identity and form a mentality not original to themselves but rather subject to the ideas of others.

As individuals look up to the elders in their life who come from similar demographics, they often feel they must take similar life paths. This is only reinforced by society's need to classify and sort people, and sometimes civil disobedience accompanies this. Following one's heritage is not always bad, but one must consider how stereotypes are often used to justify bigotry. To test the influence stereotypes have, a sample group (of Technology High School students) were given a test while exposed to a false stereotype concerning gender and comparing results to a control group. The test was measured by the amount of time taken. Those who were told negative stereotypes performed at 83% of the speed and those told positive stereotypes performed at 112% the control speed. Delving into why a population does this is imperative to grasp a better understanding of effects of stereotypes in modern day society.

Key Words: Gender, Stereotypes, Testing

INTRODUCTION

Just as it is natural for humans to assume that other cars will stop at a red light, it is natural for the human mind to categorize what is seen every day in order to focus on other events, and this does include the actions and characteristics of other humans. While it is true that a driver would have no observable evidence that the car will stop, they would assume since the vast majority of vehicles had not run the red light that any given car will not run the red light. This is what's known as cognitive efficiency. Cognitive efficiency (CE) is generally defined as qualitative increases in knowledge gained in relation to the time and effort invested in knowledge acquisition (Hoffman 2012). It does somebody no good to worry that the car might run the red light, as the probability of it is so low. Yes, this does not seem harmful until it is applied to a different subject in a negative or inaccurate light. However, with the cars, it is a vast majority rather than a slim majority and when considering other stereotypes often there is no majority. When applied to separate subjects, especially sentient humans, an ever-changing species, we often misconstrue what they actually are in order to preserve cognitive efficiency.

In layman's terms, a stereotype is a consensual belief about a group that may misrepresent an individual in said group (Gerrig 2002). We divide the world in order to stop us from being frightened. Ambivalence is not a welcome feeling when it comes to other humans and so they fill these gaps with qualities they have seen exhibited by others within a similar demographic assuming that they would act in a similar manner. This categorization of people is incredibly dangerous as each human is unique. We split the outside world into good or bad, heroes or villains, and true or false, in order to eradicate any ambiguity about the subject being observed (Lindsay 2000). This not only causes for misconceptions, but also effects, usually in a negative manner, the subject.

Our need to do this is only reinforced by the out-group homogeneity effect. The out-group homogeneity basically states that within a group, be it a tribe, state, or country, that those inside the group are diverse while those outside of it are similar (Linda 1997). Those outside of their group are more homogenous than the ones within their have displayed diversity. An example of this would be a woman in a big city thinking that all those who live in farm towns or in the country are not intelligent, while she thinks that those who live in the city can be stupid, intelligent, or somewhere in between (Alleydog). However, with our ever more connected world, those who are subject to a stereotype know about this stereotype. If those subject to it believe that it is credible, they may begin acting the way the stereotype describes solely because they feel that they ought to be that way (Linda 1997). This is known as a self-fulfilling stereotype [See Figure 1]. If a false belief about one's group is held, it can self-perpetuate through itself (Skrypnek 1982). This can be seen in testing scenarios for women or minorities. When reminded of or exposed to these stereotypes, they frequently did not perform as well at the test. It is evident that such an attitude is incredibly dangerous.

So where do these stereotypes come from? Are they rooted in our heads from our birth or are they implemented through a society? While there is no denying that the brains of men and women are wired differently through the evolutionary process, one must be wary that many of the gender roles today originate from history and have no place in a modern day society. Often people will equate correlation and causation when there is no such connection. A study done in the year of 1992 studied how 24, 30, and 36-month-old children responded to gender labeling based upon their mothers' sex-role attitudes (Fagot 1992). The older children consistently exhibited gender-based selections akin to what society's opinion is more often. Children were classified as either passing or failing the test based upon the agreeability with society. Eighty percent of the 36-month-olds, fifty percent of the 30-month olds, and ten percent of the 24-month olds passed the test. It is important to note that both the boys and girls passed the test at a similar rate. The results were fairly similar to what you would expect when you take into account that before 24-30 months children have very little to no contact with the outside world. Even when we begin going to school to learn and interact with other children, the main influence in our life is our parents (Linda 1997). In the test mentioned above, children who passed the test had mothers who gave a more traditional response on the "The Attitudes toward Women Scale" (AWS). It is unlikely that the child actually observed the actions of other children and made these correlations but rather got the ideas from their mother or father.

However, it is not only children that make the mistake of relying on only one source. Along with this absolutism of dividing the world into two, the out-group homogeneity effect is ever increasing. People reduce their news sources to these evidently biased organizations from anyone who understands that some demographics just cannot be divided into black and white. These news sources do not tell both sides of an issue. When examining a source, one must always acknowledge the reason the source is there at all. We tend to create false dichotomies, and then try to argue them using two entirely false sets of assumptions. Tim Minchin, a satirical songwriter, had an interesting analogy to creating these false dichotomies. He said that doing this is like two tennis players attempting to win a match hitting beautiful shots on opposite sides of two different tennis courts. No matter how much information there may be known for one side, if the other side is not known, it is a useless argument. We must strive to see the other side.

This idea of the genders being separated through their interests dates back to before written history. Women were considered the gatherers and the men the hunters. While the roles clearly have developed, up until the emergence of humanist ideas the dichotomies created were still prevalent in society (Rebecca 1976) and still are today, albeit much more subtle. In primary school, however, the results from the aforementioned test are exhibited. It was observed that even on the playground girls participating in what were considered boyish activities (eg. Basketball, Kickball, Soccer) were generally frowned upon unless the girl was talented at that activity. The same discrimination occurred when boys went to participate in more girly activities (Thorne 1993). This clearly is not inherent activity for boys and girls to be doing and is at least in some respect influenced by society.

All of this may seem rather insignificant if you are not subject to many stereotypes yourself. While it is true that no group is without its stereotypes, minorities are much more likely to be subjected to stereotypes. It is not even necessary that they are a minority on a national level but rather only a minority in a field in which that stereotype would then be applied (Linda 1997). For example, at the beginning of computer science the amount of men and women in the field were close to equal. Then, when the technology progressed enough and video games began, they were targeted at the male population. Then, girls got the message that computer science, and computers as a whole were not meant for them and within the next 7-8 years, the amount of women within these fields plummeted [Figure 2].

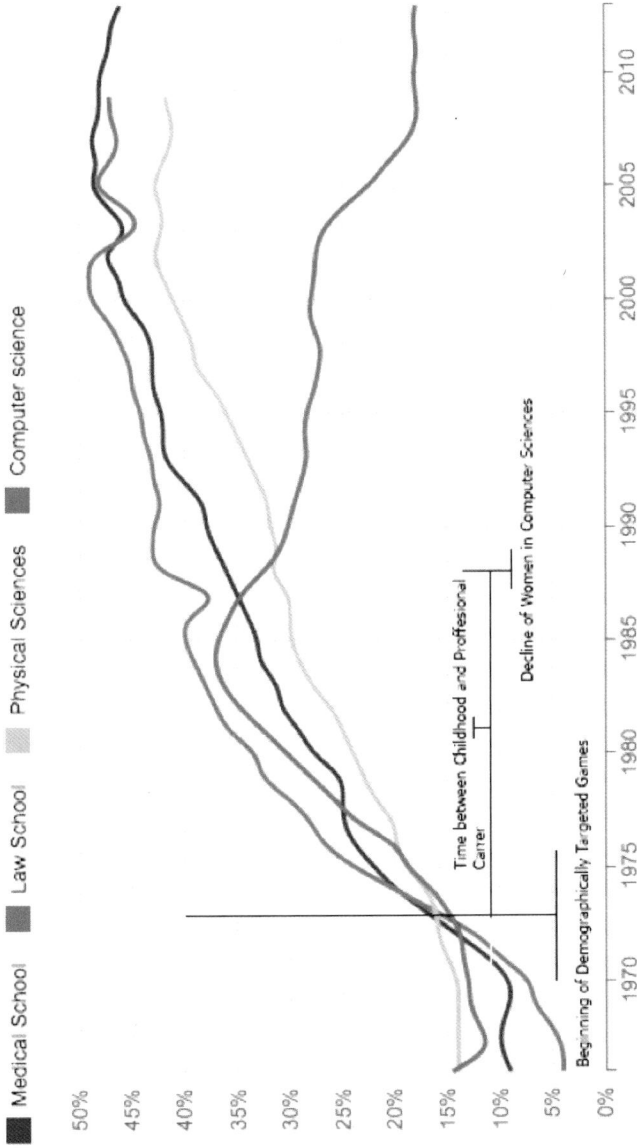

Figure 2

Not only have we seen a decline of women in computer science, but also a decline in large STEM fields. Women dominate 4 of the 5 lowest paying majors. So the data begs the question, why are women complied to join these majors rather than the engineering majors? Measuring and reducing the influence of stereotypes within a testing environment is imperative. Measuring the influence inside of testing environments is even more imperative as to not bias any of the results and to create the most accurate results possible.

MATERIALS AND METHODS

SUBJECT SELECTION

All of the subjects were recruited from Technology High School, which lies within Sonoma State University's borders. Tech High is an interesting anomaly that exemplifies some of the stereotypes within our society regarding gender. As the name demonstrates, the school centers on Science, Engineering, Math, and Technology [STEM]. As demonstrated before, society has deemed that men generally fill these STEM positions and women are expected to undertake more artistic or care-taking oriented careers.. Tech High is a magnet school in the sense that there are more applicants than the school can admit. The male population sits around 60% and the female population around 40%. This difference increases the higher the grade level appears due to an attempt to balance the genders within the school but not receiving enough female applicants.

There were 48 subjects for the test, 12 from each freshman, sophomore, junior, and senior class. Within each grade level, there were six women tested and six men. Further within that parameter, two of each gender were exposed to a positive stereotype (Their gender was better at the test), two of each gender were exposed to a negative stereotype (Their gender was worse at the test), or there was no mention at all of the performance based upon gender.

TEST SELECTION

In an attempt to avoid previously exposed stereotypes about a test, a test had to be selected in which the subjects likely had not been tested before or that which society had already previously constructed stereotypes. As well as this, the test needed a separate aspect attributed to it so that people would not discuss the test outside of the testing area. To fulfill such requirements, a test surrounding the Stroop effect was developed. The Stroop effect looks into how the brain receives conflicting information by presenting a word describing a color (eg. Yellow) but then would paint that word a separate color (Cohen 1990). Test subjects would then be asked to name the paint color overcoming the name of the color. It would seem to an average person reasonable that either males or females could exceed in this test because of women's enhanced perception of color; or perhaps they might think men would do better with a more engineering mindset, and thus being able to better separate the conflicting information.

A test mimicking the Stroop effect was created using only primary colors (eg. Red, Yellow, Blue) to distinguish and ensure that any hesitation would be caused by separating the colors rather than coming up with the proper name for the color. Instead of instructing the subjects to not discuss the test, another component was added. The actual test didn't differ at all, but at the end of the test each subject was asked if they perceived true randomness or if they thought that a human came up with the combinations of the colors. This allowed for there to be no speculation of the true variable that was being tested. Another major benefit of the test was that it was easy to measure accurately as people would always correct themselves when they got a color wrong.

EXECUTION

Each of the test subjects were tested in the relatively mellow environment of the SSU commons. This area consists of many tables and chairs and is usually sparsely populated. Unlike the library, it would allow for the speakers to speak audibly and concisely without worrying about distracting other students. Each student would sit down, separated from the others as the test subjects were usually brought in groups and handed blank cards (3" x 5" index cards) upside down.

In this time period, the stereotype was introduced. While they were holding the cards, they were told something akin to "Their gender does much better on this test" or "Their gender does much worse on this test" unless it was a control test. It was important that mentioning this was subtle but still got the point across. There were actually a couple of cases in which the subject pointed out that the statement might affect the manner in which other subjects would perform. The test was carried out as to avoid any outside discussion of the subject and the results not included with the main group.

The subjects were then asked to flip over the cards and say the color of the text aloud and then flip to the next card. This process went smoothly through all 20 of the cards and their times recorded. Due to the nature of the test, the accuracy was not an issue, as people would quickly correct themselves if they said the wrong color. As the test was the amount of time taken, this seemed like a reasonable penalty. After the test, each participant was asked about the perceived randomness of the test as to distract from the real purpose of the test. Then the participant was dismissed and asked to call in the next one.

RESULTS

For such an arduous process, when all the data were collected and consolidated, there were only two main data points. Those who were told that their gender performed better completed the task 112%

faster than the control group. Those who were told that their gender performed worse completed the task 83% of the speed of the control group. Unexpectedly, this speed difference was incredibly consistent between the two genders and the slim differences that did exist likely could be contributed to anomalies within the testing.

Unfortunately, as this experiment was done in months previous to the writing of this paper, much of the data was lost in the process of consolidation as the original data points were not taken on an electronic device but rather a separate set of papers that were not kept after the original presentation. Though they may be hasty generalizations, much of the patterns exhibited in testing were noted of and should at least be mentioned.

As to fulfill the curiosity that has likely arisen, it appeared that women actually were slightly better at the test within the control test as well as those in the Senior and Junior classes performing faster. However, this test was not meant to measure who was actually better at the test, but who was affected by the implemented stereotypes. Women were influenced more by the implemented stereotype and the aforementioned subjects that pointed out that the stereotypes might influence the test were both women. The standard deviation between the times of the women was considerably larger than that of the men. Another thing to mention is that it seemed regardless of the age of the subject, the amount affected by the stereotype ended with approximately the same amount of change in terms of percentage as the older students performed better than the younger. Once again, any slim differences between the genders could be contributed to anomalies within the testing.

DISCUSSION

Throughout the test, it was evident that society's perception, or in this case and inserted false perception, of the subject, played a large role in how the subject perceived their own ability on the test, be it consciously or subconsciously. Consequently, when applied to the real world it's easy to see how this may be detrimental in our high schools or any learning institution for that matter. It is imperative that we do our best to eliminate these generalizations in our schools and our society. But is it really only social conditioning that explains vocational preferences for each gender? Looking again at women in computer sciences, it would appear that it is the sole influence, but one must consider that there are inherent evolutionary differences between men and women. Now, it is impossible to ask the vocational preferences of newborns, but we still can notice any intrinsic differences between the genders. When measured on the Brazelton Neonatal Behavioral Assessment Scale (NBAS), newborn girls acted much differently than newborn boys (Boatella-Costa 1983).

In analyzing any data involving human subjects, one must look at the demographic that is being tested. In this case, students from Technology High School most likely don't reflect the population as accurately as possible. Even in the name, Technology High School shows that it is geared towards STEM careers. As a student that goes there, it is clear that there are no intrinsic differences in intelligence between the women and men that go there but men make up 63% of the student population and women only 37% (GreatSchools 2013). It is important to note that this is of 2013. Since, the female population has increased. It's clear that even before high school, vocational preferences are developed. When such topics arise women, and sometimes men, would mention that their parents forced them to go to Technology High School due to it being much more esteemed than its counterpart in the city. It is clear that the demographic within Technology High School is unique and may have affected the testing despite it not having the subject be related to STEM careers at all.

Reviewing our evolutionary history, it is easy to see why males would be drawn more to jobs that require brute force. Men now will often seek jobs that require more strength. Often those jobs will put their workers in more danger. In fact, 93% of workplace deaths are men instead of women (National Census 2013). This may explain part of the preference of women towards artistic, creative, or caretaking careers. However, a claim that all of the segregation between the genders in jobs is solely intrinsic would be an unfounded one.

Whereas examining our written history, a very different story is told. Women were not only treated as inferior to men, but sometimes even as property of men. Even when such ideas of property were eradicated, men were considered those who went out to provide for the family and women those who stayed home and took care of the children. However, in a modern day society these roles are unnecessary and therefore shouldn't be advocated for but rather demonstrate equality between the genders. However, like most stereotypes, this one is self-perpetuating and dangerous [Figure 1].

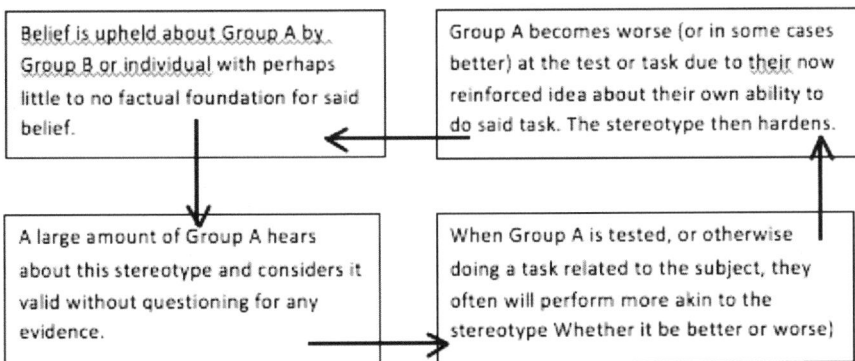

Figure 1 – How stereotypes perpetuate

How society perceives a certain demographic dictates, to a certain degree, the desires of those subject to that perception and the likelihood of pursuing any interest of that subject. Returning to the women in computer science example, people will perceive men to be much better at math and women to be generally disinterested in the subject as a whole. This is often used to justify the fact that there are not as many women in computer science as one would guess. While there is a miniscule difference between the two genders, it is not nearly enough to justify the large differences within the population [Figure 3].

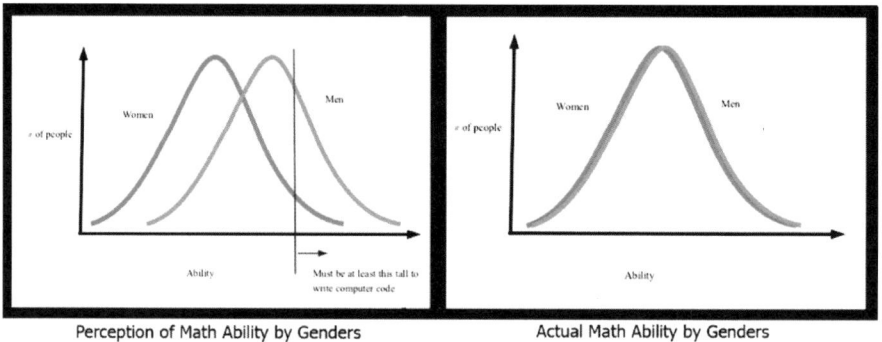

Perception of Math Ability by Genders   Actual Math Ability by Genders

Figure 3
Source: Oda, Terri SlideShare Oct 17 2009
"How does biology explain the low numbers of women in computer science?
Hint: it doesn't."

This could cause for those who are more qualified for a certain job to lose it to someone less qualified solely due to a minor discrepancy that is exaggerated in the eyes of the employer. People often accept stereotypes at face value and do not think critically about the rhetoric that is being presented to them. A stereotype does not require any veracity in order for it to be mindlessly followed by the next generation [See Figure 1]. When people do not think critically about a stereotype that is put in front of them and instead disregard it with statements such as "well stereotypes exist for a reason", they are allowing them to self-perpetuate.

CONCLUSION

It is clear that stereotypes are created through hasty generalizations. They enormously affect those who are subject to the stereotype in usually a negative manner. Even in the cases in which it would effect a demographic positively, it usually affects those who are not within that demographic in a negative manner. Allowing such invalid classification of our citizens may cause us to lose great scientists or artists. For every example of women being excluded from certain life paths, there are men that are excluded from a corresponding life path. There are many strategies and ways that have been proposed to help eradicate these stereotypes but in the end, it matters the mindset of the general populous. As long as people do not understand the diversity of other human beings, stereotypes will persist in society.

FUTURE RESEARCH

As previously discussed, the demographic that was experimented on was unique and a similar experiment done on a more diverse and larger sample size may draw results that are more conclusive. Also, a study done following individuals throughout their life and their changes based off of the stereotypes they are exposed to. The focus of this study was very limited inside a very broad topic that has near endless aspects that need to be looked into, as it very clearly is detrimental to society and those subject to stereotypes.

REFERENCES

Boatella-Costa, E., Costas-Moragas, C., Botet-Mussons, F., Fornieles-Deu, A., & Cáceres-Zurita, M. (n.d.). Behavioral gender differences in the neonatal period according to the Brazelton scale. *Early Human Development, 83*(2), 91-97. Retrieved April 10, 2015.

Fagot, Beverly I., Mary D. Leinbach, and Cherie O'Boyle. "Gender Labeling, Gender Stereotyping, and Parenting Behaviors." Developmental Psychology 28.2 (1992): 225-30. Web. Mar 2015.

Gerrig, R., & Zimbardo, P. (2002, January 1). Glossary of Psychological Terms. Retrieved April 7, 2015, from http://www.apa.org/research/action/glossary.aspx?tab=18

Great Schools -Technology High School. 2013 (n.d.). Retrieved April 11, 2015, from http://www.greatschools.org/california/rohnert-park/12248-Technology-High-School/details/

.Linda. "Stereotypes." MSU. Michigan State University, 27 Aug. 97. Web. 19 Mar. 2015. <https://www.msu.edu/course/psy/442/stereotypes.ppt>.

Martin, G. J., & Yurukoglu, A. (2014). *Bias in Cable News: Real Effects and Polarization* (No. w20798). National Bureau of Economic Research.

NATIONAL CENSUS OF FATAL OCCUPATIONAL INJURIES IN 2013. Bureau of Labor Statistics (2014, September 11). Retrieved April 11, 2015.

Oda, T. (2009, October 17). How does biology explain the low numbers of women in computer science... Retrieved April 12, 2015, from http://www.slideshare.net/terriko/how-does-biology-explain-the-low-numbers-of-women-in-cs-hint-it-doesnt

Outgroup Homogeneity Effect. (n.d.). In *Alleydog.com's online glossary*. Retrieved from: http://www.alleydog.com/glossary/definition-cit.php?term=Outgroup Homogeneity Effect

Rebecca, M., Hefner, R. and Oleshansky, B. (1976), A Model of Sex-Role Transcendence. Journal of Social Issues, 32: 197–206 Web. 23 Mar. 2015

Skrypnek, Berna J., and Mark Snyder. "On the Self-Perpetuating Nature of Stereotypes about Women and Men." *Journal of Experimental Social Psychology* 18.3 (1982): 277-91. Web. 20 Mar. 2015.

"TABLE 33. Computer Sciences Degrees Awarded, by Degree Level and Sex of Recipient: 1966–2010." (n.d.): n. pag. *National Science Foundation*. Web. 10 Mar. 2015.

Thorne, Barrie. Gender Play: Girls and Boys in School. New Brunswick, NJ: Rutgers UP, 1993. Print.

DO CHILDHOOD TRAUMAS RESULT IN ADULT DISORDERS? CELEBRITY CASE STUDIES

MOLLY MELVILLE

SOPHOMORE

TECHNOLOGY HIGH SCHOOL

ABSTRACT

The purpose of this research is to identify whether or not there is a connection between traumatic experiences in childhood and the development of an eating disorder through studying both mental illness as well as the lives of various celebrities such as Audrey Hepburn, Jane Fonda, and Princess Diana of Wales, all of whom experienced traumatic incidences in their early childhoods. Despite the setbacks of mental illness that these women, along with many others, have faced, they made huge strides towards various accomplishments in their lives. In many ways, mental illness is overshadowed and overlooked as a non-struggle being faced by only a small portion of today's generation; however, many are put into the position of struggling beneath this metaphorical silent giant of a mental illness that is so incredibly stigmatized by our society. My research focuses on anorexia and bulimia nervosa, as well as post-traumatic stress disorder, and assesses their connection to one another. Using the lives of well-known celebrities to support the connection between eating disorders and post-traumatic stress disorder, I provide a clearer view and understanding for the general public to be able to relate to.

Key Words: Audrey Hepburn, celebrity, eating disorders, post-traumatic stress disorder

On the 4th of May, 1929, Audrey Kathleen van Heemstra Ruston, later known as the actress Audrey Hepburn, was born to Ella van Heemstra and Joseph Ruston in Ixelles, Belgium. From a very young age Audrey was in love with ballet, and as she began to age, she disliked her body more and more because it looked nothing like the slender, perfect figures of ballerinas. In the words of Audrey herself, "I had an enormous complex about my looks. I thought I was ugly and I was afraid nobody would ever marry me" (Paris, 1996). Her parents sent Audrey to an English boarding school at the age of five where she began professional ballet training and continued this training through the divorce of her parents.

Described as "the most traumatic event" in her life, the disappearance of her father from their life was a tragedy from which she never truly recovered. Audrey later spoke of this tragedy in an interview where she stated, "If I could have just seen him regularly, I would have felt he loved me, and I would have felt I had a father. But as it was, I always envied other people's fathers, came home with tears, because they had a daddy." (Paris, 1996). As her parents' divorce finalized in 1938, World War II began to break out and Audrey was taken back to Holland by her mother, who believed that London was going to be bombed. As she boarded one of the last planes to leave England, Audrey saw her father for the final time.

During the war, Audrey and her mother lived with little food and heat, much like the rest of the Dutch population, despite their titles of nobility; and, although her mother never declared a pro or anti-Nazi stance, her father was imprisoned as an English Nazi supporter. After the Nazis occupied Holland, Audrey was subjected to terrible acts of violence against the Dutch people by the Nazi troops, and she vividly remembers one instance where she "saw young men put against the wall and shot" (Paris, 1996) on a frequent basis. In addition to this killing of young, Dutch men, many, including Audrey's brother Ian, were "enlisted" to work as forced labor in the German war industry.

Although she was never officially diagnosed with any mental disorder to the knowledge of the public, many speculated about her suffering from anorexia, depression, and post-traumatic stress disorder. Anorexia nervosa is a syndrome categorized by the unyielding pursuit of a thin or ideal body. However, it is not the only version of disordered eating that plagues so many young individuals; among the others are both binge eating as well as bulimia nervosa, which involves the binging and purging of large quantities of food. While this paper will not focus on the depression aspect of Audrey's mental state, it does draw conclusions connecting her post-traumatic stress brought on by suffering through the war to the eating disorder she developed in late adolescence. Post-traumatic stress disorder is characterized by the insistent mental and emotional stress sufferers' face as a result of severe psychological shock. It is hypothesized that people who have had or currently suffer from an eating disorder (ED) have much higher correlation or rates of self-reported traumatization and post-traumatic stress disorder, and this can be supported by the lives of several celebrities such as the previously mentioned Audrey Hepburn, actress Jane Fonda, and the previous princess of Wales, Diana.

First brought into the public eye in relation to veterans of war, post-traumatic stress syndrome, or PTSD, can develop as a result of a huge variety of traumatic incidents (National Institute of Mental Health, n.d.). Characterized by the sufferers' extreme mental and emotional stress, PTSD will affect nearly 8% of the US population sometime in their lives, and affects women at twice the rate of men (Nebraska Department of Veterans' Affairs, 2007). The symptoms experienced by PTSD sufferers' can be group into three categories: re-experiencing symptoms, which often interrupt the daily routine of a person's life; avoidance symptoms, which may cause a person to change their daily routine; and hyperarousal symptoms, which make daily tasks difficult to complete (National Institute of Mental Health, n.d.). While it is obvious that PTSD is caused by a traumatic experience, scientists are making further research in regards to both the genes behind PTSD, as well as the areas of the brain that are most affected by the trauma. Living with PTSD can have severe impacts on a persons' daily life, and, in addition to this, may cause the person to make difficult changes to their routine.

As previously stated, PTSD affects the way in which its sufferers' function through three subgroups of symptoms. The first of these subgroups, re-experiencing symptoms, are the reliving of the traumatic event and can impact a persons' everyday routine severely. Sufferers' undergo terrifying flashbacks, which can include a racing heartbeat and sweating, as well as bad dreams and frightening thoughts in relation to the trauma (National Institute of Mental Health, n.d.). Avoidance symptoms, typically characterized by the avoidance of triggers relating to the trauma, including staying away from triggering places or objects, as well as felling numbness, guilt, depression, or worry; these symptoms also include a loss of memory around the traumatic event and can cause a person to go out of their way to change normal routine in order to avoid triggers. The third and final subgroup of PTSD symptoms are the hyperarousal symptoms which include: hypersensitivity, insomnia, and tenseness; these symptoms often make it difficult to easily complete daily tasks such as eating or concentrating. Although these symptoms may be apparent in non-PTSD sufferers, they characterize the diagnosis of PTSD if they last for more than a few weeks or months.

Although PTSD is triggered through a traumatic event, many people contain predispositions to suffer from the disorder that many others may not develop after a trauma occurs. Research from the University of California: Los Angeles shows that there are two genes associated with higher serotonin production, which can lead to a higher risk at obtaining PTSD (Shepherd, 2012). According to Dr. Armen Goenjian, lead author of the study and research professor of psychiatry, "People can develop post-traumatic stress disorder after surviving a life-threatening ordeal like war, rape or a natural disaster... If confirmed, our findings could eventually lead to new ways to screen people at risk for PTSD and target specific medicines for preventing and treating the disorder" (Schmidt, 2012). In addition to this possibly genetic predisposition of PTSD, the other large factor in deciding how a person responds to a traumatic event lies in the way their brain responds to different signals. These brain areas include the amygdala, hippocampus, and prefrontal cortex, and studies show that patients with PTSD have smaller hippocampal volumes (Bremner, 2006). In addition to this discovery, the studies show that people, especially women, who suffered from childhood abuse-related PTSD had high levels of hypercortisolemia, in contrast to those with normal baseline Cortisol levels who suffered from sexual abuse as adults (Lemieux & Coe, 1995).

Post-traumatic stress disorder is a serious mental illness that affects a person's daily life; in addition to this, it can also lead to the development of various other mental illnesses as the result of a weakened psyche and genetic predispositions. Some of the more common disorders PTSD sufferers' are prone to include panic disorder, obsessive-compulsive disorder, and social phobia (Cohen, 2006). According to Harold Cohen, Ph.D., people who have suffered from trauma in childhood, and develop adult PTSD as a result, are often more likely to develop irregular behavior patterns or traits and be treated for borderline personality disorders such as the ones stated above. These disorders, however, can also be linked to the development of an eating disorder, especially in young women. Many of the factors that spur PTSD can also jumpstart the development of an eating disorder in a person who is already predisposed to the condition or who may have previously suffered from it.

Characterized by extreme thoughts, emotions, and behaviors surrounding weight and food, an eating disorder can have serious emotional and physical consequences for the sufferer, and has the highest mortality rate of any mental illness. Complications, or "symptoms", of eating disorders include: abnormal heart beats, anxiety, fatigue, irregular menstrual cycles in women, and drug or alcohol abuse. There are multiple reasons a person may suffer from an eating disorder, though there is no absolute causation; a few of the factors that play a substantial role in the development of an eating disorder include genetics, biological factors, and cultural pressure (Simon, 2013). The start of an eating disorder is often triggered through some sort of life altering event such as the start of puberty or a move out of state. A person is not defined by their disorders, but the way in which a person's mind works does have an effect on the way in which they conduct their lives.

Eating disorders are commonly misunderstood by the general public, who often blame the illness on society's constant message to be thin. However, most who develop an eating disorder were predisposed to the illness through a hereditary gene, and the triggering event that can set off the disorder is often completely unavoidable. Although eating disorders were traditionally treated as a result of social or cultural pressures, it is now understood to be a developmental or biological illness and is treated as such, focusing on the genetics behind it rather than the outside pressures faced (Collier & Treasure, 2004). To further support this theory, studies have been conducted involving identical twins who suffer from anorexia nervosa; however, it is not possible to determine the exact genes responsible for the development of an eating disorder (Collier & Treasure, 2004). They are often triggered by large-scale changes in a person's life or hormones, such as puberty, starting college, the ending or beginning of a relationship, and occasionally pregnancy. An eating disorder can also begin through the experiencing of a traumatic experience, much like PTSD, and both take root in genetic footholds or predisposition.

Although not determinant of each other, PTSD and eating disorders are undoubtedly related, as both are mental illness brought on by extreme circumstances or changes in a person's life. According to a study done by the Department of Social Science, Abo Akademi University, "trauma history in ED patients merits attention" as the results suggest that traumas are linked to higher rates of EDs, regardless of ED or trauma type (Backholm, Isomaa, & Birgegard, 2013). In another study done in Rome, Italy, it was stated that "several studies have shown that physical and/or sexual abuse during childhood may lead to the development of obesity later in life" (D'Argenio, et al., 2009). Although obesity has not been discussed thus far in the research, it is a type of disordered eating habit known as binge eating; binge eating disorder is more thoroughly discussed in a paper from the Department of Neurosciences, University of Padova, Italy. Although D'Argenio's paper fails to discuss the rates of eating disorders in any form, it does focus on the impact of a stressful life event and the development of a binge eating disorder versus the development of bulimia nervosa; both disorders are higher than a lack of one, but the results were inconclusive in determining the rate at which people suffer the different diseases (Degortes, et al., 2014). Experiencing a trauma, whether it is war or the death of a loved one, can take a huge mental and emotional toll on a person; eating disorders are often born out of the strong desire to have control over one's life, when so many other factors are spinning completely out of control.

Audrey Hepburn suffered immensely from World War II, but was never treated for or diagnosed with any kind of mental disorder or disturbance. However, throughout her life it was speculated that she had both post-traumatic stress disorder, accompanied by depression, and anorexia nervosa or possibly bulimia nervosa. In a 1990 Phil Donahue interview, Audrey admitted that "If I get nervous, I don't eat", which was brought on by speculation regarding her currently underweight frame. This notion of an eating disorder was only further supported by the idea that "she would never fully recover from the war" and the known fact that "she later deprived herself of, or felt she could do without, food" (Paris, 1996). The war, as it is now understood, played a huge developmental role in Audrey's life and may have resulted in PTSD and the related ED. While no one will never be sure of the illnesses suffered by Audrey throughout her life, it is possible to make assumptions based upon what information is known, in collaboration with the stories of various others who suffered a huge trauma and later struggled with disordered eating.

The remarkable story of Jane Fonda is one of these, as her mother slit her throat when Jane was only 12 (Bosworth, 2011). Some describe this as the most influential moment in Jane's life, as she had already been struggling for the affection of her unattached father, Henry Fonda. After dropping out of Vassar College, Fonda suffered from an eating disorder for a total of 25 years, during which she became both a model and renowned actress. In an interview with Amanda de Cadenet, she admitted this fact as well as the acknowledgment of her nervous breakdown in which she came to the realization of accepting religion, despite being raised an atheist. Jane's openness to talking about and discussing her struggle has provided less speculation and in-depth research than the illness surrounding Audrey Hepburn, but it is incredibly notable and intriguing as she has behaved much more openly pertaining to interest in her mental health. Her story only further supports the theory that extreme trauma in childhood, such as the suicide of a parent or the witnessing of a war, can have an effect much later in life, and that effect can occur in the development of an eating disorder.

Unlike the other two cases discussed in this report, the story of Princess Diana of Wales is much less dramatic and therefore traumatic. She grew up in a life of luxury, as a member of a British noble family, but suffered through the divorce of her parents and the disappearance of her mother from her life. The divorce, finalized in 1969, had a resounding effect on Diana, who blatantly said, "I will never marry unless I'm really in love because if you're not in love, you're going to get divorced – and I never intend to be divorced" (Keck, 2007). Throughout the remainder of her childhood, Diana dreamed of being happily married with a large family (Keck, 2007). According to Lady Colin Campbell, when Diana was prepping for her wedding in 1981, a condition of bulimia surfaced (Di's Private Battle, 1992). This source claims that upon seeing herself plumping up in engagement photos, Diana began a strict diet and ultimately broke this to begin a vicious cycle of binging and purging. Shockingly, Prince Charles' biographer, Penny Junor, "claims that Diana's troubled childhood is the cause of her eating disorder" (Di's Private Battle, 1992). This claim from a royal insider only further supports the idea of relation between childhood traumas, such as the one Diana was subjected to, and eating disorders later in life.

While all three of these celebrities suffered from different sources of trauma, they each underwent their own external pain and found themselves as grown women with an obsessive nature characterized by the development of an eating disorder. It can be interpreted that there is strong association between trauma history, post-traumatic stress disorder, and the development of other mental illnesses, most specifically disordered eating. These connections are based on societal pressures, but take a firm hold within the genetics and brains of each individual. Through examining both scientific texts concerning the relationship between trauma and EDs and the lives of various celebrities who suffered through both, a comprehensible union was established and will hopefully, be further researched in years to come.

References

Backholm, K., Isomaa, R., & Birgegard, A. (2013). The prevalence and impact of trauma history in eating disorder patients. *European Journal of Psychotraumatology*, 1-9.

Bosworth, P. (2011). *Jane Fonda: The Private Life of a Public Woman*. New York: Biteback Publishing.

Bremner, J. D. (2006). Traumatic stress: effects on the brain. *Dialogues in clinical neuroscience*. Retrieved March 19, 2015, from http://www.ncbi.nlm.nih.gov/pmc/articles/PMC3181836/

Cohen, H. (2006). *Associated Conditions of PTSD*. Retrieved March 19, 2015, from PsychCentral: http://psychcentral.com/lib/associated-conditions-of-ptsd/000157

Collier, D. A., & Treasure, J. L. (2004, October 29). The aetiology of eating disorders. *The British Journal of Psychiatry, 185*(5). doi:10.1192/185.5.363

D'Argenio, A., Mazzi, C., Pecchioli, L., Di Lorenzo, G., Siracusano, A., & Troisi, A. (2009). Early trauma and adult obesity: Is psychological dysfunction the mediating mechanism? *Physiology & Behavior*, 543-546.

Degortes, D., Santonastaso, P., Zanetti, T., Tenconi, E., Veronese, A., & Favaro, A. (2014). Stressful Life Events and Binge Eating Disorder. *European Eating Disorders Review*, 378-382.

Di's Private Battle. (1992, August 3). *People Magazine, 38*(5).

Keck, K. (2007, August 17). Nannies tell new details of Princess Diana's childhood. *CNN*.

Lemieux, & Coe. (1995). Abuse-related posttraumatic stress disorder: evidence for chronic neuroendocrime activation in women. *Psychosom Med.*, 105-15.

National Institute of Mental Health. (n.d.). *Post-Traumatic Stress Disorder (PTSD)*. (National Institutes of Health) Retrieved March 18, 2015, from National Institute of Mental Health:

http://www.nimh.nih.gov/health/topics/post-traumatic-stress-disorder-ptsd/index.shtml

Nebraska Department of Veterans' Affairs. (2007). *Post Traumatic Stress Disorder*. Retrieved March 18, 2015

Paris, B. (1996). *Audrey Hepburn.* New York: G. P. Putnam's Sons.

Schmidt, E. (2012, April 2). *UCLA study identifies genes linked to post-traumatic stress disorder*. Retrieved from UCLA Newsroom: http://newsroom.ucla.edu/releases/ucla-study-identifies-first-genes-231248

Shepherd, R. (2012, April 3). *Post-Traumatic Stress Disorder Linked To Genetics*. Retrieved from Medical News Today: http://www.medicalnewstoday.com/articles/243717.php

Simon, H. (2013, June 24). *Eating disorders.* Retrieved from University of Maryland Medical Center: http://umm.edu/health/medical/reports/articles/eating-disorders

A Variety of Plants Growth in Respect to the Diversification of Growing Methods and Enhancers

ZACHARY MILLER

JUNIOR

TECHNOLOGY HIGH SCHOOL

ABSTRACT

My first hypothesis was the concept that worms could affect the soil pH, and plant height. To test this, I used three different plants for my experiment, namely Onion plants, Primroses, and Snapdragons. My results were that the pH level in the soil rose when the number of worms rose, and that between 5-7 worms was most effective. My second series of experiments was if the fertilizer amount recommended was most beneficial, and whether companion planting was beneficial to plants. Testing my hypothesis, I used Pac Toi and Kale Scarlet plants, planted 6 pairs of them, and planted 3 of each separately. I acquired fertilizer, and poured it on half of the pairs, and then let the other half grow normally. I then planted Festuca plants, and put varying fertilizer amounts on them. The recommended amount of fertilizer was most beneficial, and those plants that were planted next to each other grew faster than those planted alone. My third series of experiments was whether Gibberellic Acid and Hydroponic growing methods affected growth. I acquired 4 Pansies, Alyssum, Vinca, and Sagina. 2 of each went into the Hydroponics system, and 2 grew in soil. Then, 1 of each was sprayed with acid in both experiments. The other plants in both experiments grew without any acid. My results were that those who were planted in the hydroponics system with the Gibberellic acid grew much better than any other plants. The experiments were conducted over a period of 3 years.

Key Words: Fertilizer, Natural Growth Methodology, Onions, Plants, Primroses, Snapdragons

INTRODUCTION

THE GIANT AND THE SHADOW
THE FERTILIZER AND CHEMICAL '*GIANT*'
AND THE '*SHADOW*' OF NATURAL GROWTH ENHANCERS

Plants have many different ways of growing, and therefore, can have their growth affected in many different ways. Fertilizers and chemicals have been a huge part of agricultural society today and can be considered the giant of that community. The way that they help plants grow is admirable, and due to the fact that it's well known, many people use fertilizer. However, in the shadow of the giant of fertilizer and chemicals lurk many other ways to help plants grow other than fertilizer. Diverse growing methods such as Gibberellic Acid, companion planting, hydroponic growing, and numbers of worms are all counterparts that lurk within the shadow of the "giant" of fertilizer and chemicals.

The "giant" that is known as fertilizer has many drawbacks, which makes the counterparts in the "shadow" much more desirable for us. Fertilizer and other chemicals are extremely harmful to the environment. Some chemicals can have a positive effect on a plant, but if consumed by any member of the ecosystem, it, results in death. The growth of a plant should not be related with the death of something else.

The plant hormone, Gibberellic Acid, with the chemical formula $C_{19}H_{22}O_6$ (Gibberellic Acid, 2014) was first found in Japan in 1934. (Giberrilins, 2014) The way the Japanese had found this hormone was because after noticing how tall their rice plants were growing, something was wrong. After simple tests they were able to conclude that it was Gibberellic Acid. This acid is completely natural, not brewed in a factory. It does not harm animals, humans, or the environment. In the middle of my experiment, my dogs actually drank some of the acid, and did not have any problems with it at all, so it is with he utmost certainty that I conclude that it is completely harmless. Almost every experiment, except one, was completely harmless to any animals. My desire was to find efficient way to grow plants while keeping everything surrounding the experiment, including the environment, pets, and other insects safe.

METHOD

For my first experiment, I tested whether plant growth could be affected by the amount of worms within the soil. To test this experiment, I took 11 onion plants, 11 Snapdragons, and 11 Primroses. With these plants, I had 0, 1…10 worms planted in each plant's box. I then observed the way they grew over time, and in addition observed the pH level at the start of each experiment and then viewed it again at the end. For this experiment I experimented 11 of the three said plants, a ruler for measuring, a pH level testing kit, and 165 worms. A camera or phone was needed to take photographs of the plants.

The methods for this experiment are as follows: Advance to a store and buy 11 Snapdragons, 11 Primroses, and 11 onion plants. In addition, purchase a ruler, a pH level testing kit, and acquire 165 worms. After, test the pH level of each planter box and record the data you collect. Then, take the 165 worms and divide them up into the container in consecutive numbers, starting with 0, and ending with 10. After all the worms are divvied up among the containers, plant the plants in each of the containers. Make sure that the plants are planted in their own row of consecutive numbers, that way Snapdragons, Primroses, and onion plants all are growing in the same conditions. Refer to the chart in the results section. After this is done, water daily for the first week, and then every 2 days for the 2nd and 3rd week. Measure the plants once a week, taking pictures of the plants as well, recording the data. At the end of the 3rd week, measure the pH level and compare it to the starting pH level. Draw conclusions about worms, plant growth, and pH levels after all data is collected.

For the second experiment, I tested whether companion planting and fertilizer amounts affected plant growth in a positive way. The materials needed are as follow. Miracle-Gro fertilizer, a ruler, 6 Festuca plants, 9 Pac Toi plants, and 9 Kale Scarlet plants are needed as well. A camera or phone is needed to take photographs of the plants.

Pac Toi

Hydroponics Planting System

The methods for creating a successful experiment are as follows: Advance to the store and buy Miracle-Gro fertilizer, a ruler, 6 Festuca plants, 6 Pac Toi plants, and 6 Kale Scarlet plants. When at your desired location for your experiment, plant the 6 Festuca plants several inches away from each other. Take the Miracle-Gro fertilizer and put 0 grams on the first plant. Put 3 grams on the next plant, 5 grams on the next plant, 9 grams on the next plant, 15 grams on the next plant, and 30 grams on the last plant. The recommended amount of fertilizer on the Miracle-Gro bottle is around 7 grams. Water the plants daily for 1 week, and then every 2 days for the two following weeks. Measure the plants once a week. Take the Pac Toi and Kale Scarlet and plant three of each away from each other, essentially letting them grow on their own, this will be the control variable. Take the remaining three of each plant and plant them in pairs with the opposite plant. Put the recommended amount of fertilizer (7 grams) on the pairs. For all 12 of these plants, water daily for the first week, and every 2 days for the consccutive two weeks. Record the growth data once a week, along with taking pictures of the plants. Take data and analyze which fertilizer amount works the best, and whether the combination of companion planting and fertilizer outmatched that of no enhancers on the control variable plants.

The materials used were used for two experiments. For the Hydroponic experiment I used a hydroponics system in which the plants are grown. For the dry experiment I used planter boxes with soil. From there I used one teaspoon of Gibberellic acid powder, mixed with 16 fluid ounces of water, which would be sprayed on half of the plants. It was put into a spray bottle. My other materials were 4 Pansies, 4 Saginas, 4 Vincas, and 4 Alyssums. I also used a ruler to measure the length of the plants. I used my iPhone to take pictures of the plants.

The methods to conduct a successful experiment are as follows: Advance to the store and purchase 4 Pansies, 4 Saginas, 4 Vincas, and 4 Alyssums, and purchase a hydroponics planting system. Take 2 of each plant and wash them under the sink with warm water until most of the dirt is no longer in between the roots. From there you measure the plant. Fill up the hydroponics kit with water. Put the plants in planter circle, one to a circle. Then take the other two (which haven't been washed) and plant them with a differing plant species in a planter box with soil, two to a box. There will be 4 boxes by the end; make sure the pairs are the same. Measure the plants after they are planted. Take one spoonful of the Gibberellic Acid Powder and mix it with 16 fluid ounces of water. Spray 1 Pansy, 1 Sagina, 1 Vinca, and 1 Alyssum in both the dry and hydroponic experiments with Gibberellic Acid. Make sure that all the pants affected by the acid are in the same container for the dry experiment, and for the hydroponics experiment that they are all on one side of the hydroponics system. Record growth for 9 days, while measuring the growth of the plants 6 times. After the 9 days, measure the hydroponic plants with a ruler. Then dig up the plants in the planter boxes and wash their roots with water until there is no soil left in between them. Measure the plants, including the roots. See which combination worked best for your plants.

RESULTS

The results for the three different experiments will be given in the form of charts. Each chart will then be analyzed. For space, the table for the first experiment is on the next page. My hypothesis for the first experiment was that plant growth would be affected in a positive way with worms, and that a healthy number of worms would be most helpful. I also hypothesized that with more worms, the pH level of the soil will go up. I predicted that as the pH level went up, the plant growth would be positive. It was hypothesized that each type of plant would be affected the same as well. The reason I used 3 different types of plants is because that way a diverse collection of data can be collected. The table illustrates my results for the first experiment.

In table number one, it can be concluded that between 5-7 worms was ideal for each of the plants. The "w" on the first row stands for worms. The pH level measured was much higher for these plants than for the rest. Space has prohibited me from entering in the pH level data. However, the pH level for the plants with 5-9 worms was around 7. This is much better than when the experiment was started, and the pH level was around 4. Because of the data collected, a conclusion can be drawn that an average of 5-7 worms was most effective, resulting in high plant growth and high pH levels. The high pH levels resulted in better plant growth, and those plants with less worms and lower pH levels resulted in smaller, weaker plants. Both of my hypotheses were correct.

Table 1

Plant Name	# of worms in each plant										
	0	1	2	3	4	5	6	7	8	9	10
Week #1											
Onion	3	4	4.4	3.5	6	4.1	2.5	2.7	4.7	3.2	4.6
Snapdragon	6	5.9	6.3	4.3	5	6.1	4.7	6	6.2	2	6.5
Primroses	2	2.3	3	3.4	3.3	*2.5*	2.8	3.2	4	3	2.2
Week #2											
Onion	5.2	6.5	6.3	7	6.9	8.3	9.6	8.2	5.2	4.6	5.3
Snapdragon	6.5	6.3	6.7	6.8	7	7.5	7.8	7.7	7.6	7.4	7.1
Primroses	3.4	4.2	6	5.7	6.2	7.6	8.4	8.3	7.4	6.3	5.9
Week #3											
Onion	7.9	8	7.5	7.6	8	11.2	11.3	11	7.4	6	5.8
Snapdragon	7.5	7.1	7.6	7.7	8.1	8.8	9.1	9.6	8.7	8.1	7.3
Primroses	4	4.5	6.6	6.7	6.5	7.1	7.3	7.2	6.9	6.4	6.1

The size of the worms for each week in each plant is given in inches.

Editor's note: *The tables within this paper were altered to fit space constraints. No data has been changed, merely presented in a more compact and efficient format.*

For my second experiment, I put the data in two different tables base on the two different experiments. The two experiments are the test of fertilizer amounts, and the test of fertilizer and companion planting. My hypothesis was that the recommended amount of fertilizer would be the most beneficial. My hypothesis for the second experiment was that the combination of companion planting and fertilizer would outmatch that of the plants growing on their own.

Table 2

Plant: Festuca	*Grams of Fertilizer*					
Week #	**0**	**3**	**5**	**9**	**15**	**30**
1	1 in.	1.4 in.	1.7 in.	1.6 in.	1.1 in.	0.9 in.
2	1.5 in.	1.7 in.	2.4 in.	2.5 in.	0.9 in.	0.5 in.
3	1.7 in.	2.1 in.	2.7 in.	2.4 in.	1 in.	0.5 in.

The table above shows the experiment regarding fertilizer amounts. I used the Festuca plant. After the experiment was finished I was able to conclude from the data collected that the recommended fertilizer was most beneficial for plant growth. My hypothesis for this experiment was correct.

The table for the second part of the experiment regarding companion planting and fertilizer amounts. The "PT, KS" stands for Pac Toi, and Kale Scarlet growth among the table. The first 6 rows are each of the plants growing separately with no growth enhancers. The last 6 rows of the pairs of plants are 3 plant pairs *with no fertilizer*, and then 3 pairs of plants *with fertilizer*. My hypothesis was correct in the sense that those plants with fertilizer and in pairs grew better than those alone.

For my third and final experiment, I tested whether hydroponic growing and Gibberellic Acid were beneficial to plant growth. After all the data from the experiment was collected I inputted it all into a table. My hypothesis for this experiment was that those plants that grew with water and Gibberellic acid would grow the best. The reason why there are 4 plants is because each plant grows and looks differently. A Vinca is a tall leafy plant with vines, while a Sagina is a small, wide, grassy ground cover plant. A Pansy is a tall flowery plant, while the Alyssum is a small, wide ground cover plant. This way, the results I get are coming from a variety of plants, and not the same types of plants.

Table 3

Name of Plant	Date in January							
	4	7	8	9	10	11	12	16
Hydroponic Pansies Gibberellic Acid	9.75	9.8	9.9	9.9	10	10.1	10.4	14
Hydroponics Pansies	10	10	10	10.2	10.3	10.5	10.6	12
Hydroponic Alyssums Gibberellic Acid	5.56	6	6.2	6.76	7	7.4	8	8.7
Hydroponic Alyssums	7.25	7.25	7.25	7.25	7.27	7.28	7.29	7.5
Hydroponic Saginas Gibberellic Acid	5.6	5.9	6.3	6.6	7	7.3	7.7	6.5
Hydroponic Saginas	6.6	6.6	6.6	6.6	6.7	6.7	5.7	6
Hydroponic Vincas Gibberellic Acid	11.6	11.5	11.4	11.4	11.3	11.1	11	10.5
Hydroponic Vincas	11.2	10.9	10.5	10.3	10.1	9.3	9	8.3
Dry Pansy Gibberellic Acid	4.75	5	5.3	5.6	5.7	6.1	6.4	8
Dry Pansy	5.2	5.2	5.2	5.3	5.3	5.4	5.5	8.8
Dry Alyssum Gibberellic Acid	2.7	2.7	2.7	2.8	2.9	3	3.1	8.3
Dry Alyssum	2.1	2.1	2.3	2.3	2.5	2.6	2.75	6.2
Dry Sagina Gibberellic Acid	1	1.1	1.1	1.3	1.4	1.7	2	5.5
Dry Sagina	0.75	0.75	0.8	0.8	0.8	1	1.2	5.5
Dry Vinca Gibberellic Acid	6.2	6.2	6.2	6.2	6.3	6.3	6.3	13.5
Dry Vinca	4.75	5	5	5.3	5.6	5.8	6	11.5

The table above shows the results for the third experiment. The columns illustrate the growth of the plants over time. The topmost row shows the date in which the plants were measured. Everything was measured in inches. From the results I collected I can conclude that those plants that are growing in the hydroponics system with Gibberellic acid grew the best. Although there was one instance in which the dry Vinca with Gibberellic acid grew better than that of the hydroponics system with Gibberellic acid. However, even though this occurred, 100% of the plants that grew with Gibberellic Acid grew better than those without. My hypothesis was partially correct, because only 75% of those plants in the hydroponic system grew better than those in the dry experiment with the Gibberellic acid. However, that is more than the majority.

DISCUSSION

My results for the three experiments I conducted were superb. For my first experiment, it is better to grow plants with worms than without. Growing them with the worms allows the pH level to rise. Companion planting is something that, with fertilizer, yields fantastic results. However, for this experiment, I only used vegetable plants, and, if this experiment is done again, I will use flower plants. For the third experiment, those plants that were participating in the dry experiment had a much greener plant, while the roots were much shorter. In the hydroponics system the roots were growing very well. Root growth has always been connected with good plant growth. (The Importance of Roots - Bonnie Plants, 2014) Therefore, I think, over time, the hydroponics plant would grow much taller than that of the plants in the dry experiment. In the future, I would like to take a variety of plants, placing some in dirt and others in water. The ones placed in the water would have an inert medium (gravel) placed so that worms would survive. Then I would spray fertilizer and Gibberellic Acid, while having the plants planted in pairs. This experiment would be combining all the beneficial factors in plant growth into one big compact experiment. These experiments, over the course of 3 years, have given me data that helps me understand the vast and complex way that factors affect different parts of plant growth. These experiments are ones that could change the way unnatural growing techniques are used, and change the way plants are grown in the future in general.

REFERENCES

"Gibberellic Acid for Fruit Set and Seed Germination." *Gibberellic Acid for Fruit Set and Seed Germination.* Web. 2 Oct. 2014. <http://www.crfg.org/tidbits/gibberellic.html>.

"Parthenocarpic Apple Fruit Production Conferred by Transposon Insertion Mutations in a MADS-box Transcription Factor; Www.pnas.org." *Giberrilins.* Web. 4 Nov. 2014. <http://plantcellbiology.masters.grkraj.org/html/Plant_Growth_And_Development4-Plant_Hormones-Gibberellins.htm>.

"The Importance of Roots - Bonnie Plants." *Bonnie Plants.* Web. 11 Apr. 2014. <http://bonnieplants.com/library/the-importance-of-roots/>.

AFTERWORD

KARIN ENSTAM JAFFE
PROFESSOR OF ANTHROPOLOGY
SONOMA STATE UNIVERSITY

The papers in the 2015 *Society and Culture Undergraduate Research Forum Journal* represent the culmination of one of the best academic experiences an undergraduate student can have during his/her college career: the chance to engage in independent research under the close guidance of a faculty member. The diverse topics explored in this issue, ranging from using case studies to examine whether childhood trauma results in adult disorders (Molly Melville) and a study of undocumented Latino students in higher education (Griselda Madrigal Lara), to an investigation of the effects of growing methods and enhancers on plant growth (Zachary Miller) and a study of power and privilege in everyday campus communications (Nanette Reyes Cruz), speak to the impressive results of this student-faculty research collaboration. While 'traditional' classroom instruction (i.e., lecture, in-class discussions and activities, exams, and term papers) is integral to a college education, independent research provides undergraduates with the ability to apply what they learn in the classroom and interact closely with a faculty mentor to achieve a common goal: to question, to explore, and ultimately, to understand something better.

It is the potential for this kind of academic experience that attracted me to Sonoma State as a newly-minted Ph.D. in August 2002. Coming from UC Davis, I saw first-hand how little interaction there was between faculty members and most undergraduates at a large, Ph.D.-granting university, and I wanted something different. Sonoma State offered me the opportunity to work closely with undergraduate students, both in the classroom and beyond. In fact, I was repeatedly told by colleagues that faculty research was most valued when it could be used to enhance our students' academic experience, either by bringing the research into the classroom as a teaching tool, or by involving students directly in the research itself.

This was an exciting proposition for me, and I found it relatively easy to incorporate examples from my research on the anti-predator behavior of vervet and patas monkeys in Kenya to illustrate concepts in my *Primate Behavioral Ecology* class. Involving students *actively* in research was more difficult, however, and it took me several years to develop a research agenda that could provide students with cost-effective and meaningful research experiences. I started the Sonoma State University Primate Ethology Research Lab in 2007, but it wasn't until 2013 that the lab's focus began to take shape in the form of applied ethology. Applied ethology uses the scientific principles of studying animal behavior to better understand animals living in captivity and enhance wellness. As the lab's focus narrowed, interest in the lab's research grew: students seemed to want more than a 'research experience', they wanted to know that their research was making a difference in the real world. With this applied focus, I have overseen the independent research of 15 undergraduates on a variety of research projects since April 2013. The partial results of two of these projects appear in this journal: an assessment of the core behavioral needs of captive mandrills (Kyle Runzel) and an examination of enclosure use in an all-male group of squirrel monkeys (Madeline Warnement). The results of both of these projects will be shared with the San Francisco Zoo to help inform the future care and management of these animals.

The theme for the 2015 Society and Culture Undergraduate Research Forum Journal, *Within the Shadow of Giants*, was designed by the forum organizers to "invoke the ways in which metaphorical shadows are cast upon the social, cultural, and academic environment," and to encourage students to think about how "ideas, events, or particular persons manifest themselves in the world, and inspire people to explore, create, and – ultimately, – to grow?" (2015 SCURF Organizing Committee). While undergraduates can be inspired by what they learn in the classroom (I certainly hope that my classes inspire students), this is no substitute for the inspirational effect that independent research under the close mentorship of a caring and involved faculty member can have. My hope is that Sonoma State undergraduates do not feel intimidated by the 'shadows' that they perceive faculty cast, but rather embrace the opportunities afforded to them by faculty, like myself, who truly enjoy working closely with motivated, inquisitive students and want to share the joy of asking a question, the excitement of developing a project, and the satisfaction of finding the answer and sharing it with others, as the students published in the 2015 *Society and Culture Undergraduate Research Forum Journal* have done.

PHOTOS FROM THE 7TH ANNUAL
SOCIETY & CULTURE UNDERGRADUATE RESEARCH FORUM
APRIL 15TH 2015

POSTER PRESENTATION ROOM

LONG VIEW OF THE POSTER PRESENTATION ROOM

PHOTOS FROM THE 7TH ANNUAL
SOCIETY & CULTURE UNDERGRADUATE RESEARCH FORUM
APRIL 15TH 2015

THE ANTHROPOLOGY CLUB TABLE

MEMBERS SHOWN:

DOSHIA CARADINE (LEFT)

MADISON LONG (RIGHT)

PHOTOS FROM THE 7TH ANNUAL
SOCIETY & CULTURE UNDERGRADUATE RESEARCH FORUM
APRIL 15TH 2015

SEVERAL MEMBERS OF THE
SOCIETY & CULTURE UNDERGRADUATE RESEARCH FORUM TEAM
(FROM LEFT TO RIGHT)

DOSHIA CARADINE, ALEXANDER COBURN, MADISON LONG,
AMY VILLASENOR, LAUREN RUSS, DR. ALEXIS BOUTIN